William A. Kelly

About the Author...

William A. Kelly is founder and president of Kelly Financial Services. He is a Registered Investment Advisor (RIA) and he has worked with seniors since 1994. William is a noted author and speaker and lectures nationally to various professional groups.

His articles have appeared in the Boston Herald. Inc. Magazine, USA Today, The New York Times, the Providence Journal and the Patriot Ledger, have all published articles concerning William.

William has presented business plans before the MIT Enterprise Forum in Cambridge, MA and before the Brown University Faculty Club in Providence, RI.

He has presented his Senior Safe Money Strategies(SM) workshop to more than eight thousand seniors over the past eight years.

William lives in Rhode Island with his wife, Kelly, and two daughters.

An RIA is an individual who has registered with the Securities & Exchange Commission (SEC) and holds himself out to be an investment advisor. Registration is required of anyone who, for compensation and as part of a business, gives advice, makes recommendations, issues repo or furnishes analysis of securities directly or through publications. RIA is not a credential. It simply means an individual or firm has successfully submitted certain filings to the Securities & Exchange Commission.

Senior Safe Money Strategies^(sm)

Retirement Survival for Seniors

Investment Planning and Estate Planning

William A. Kelly Publishing

William A. Kelly Financial

Copyright © 2005

ISBN-0-9665630-1-8

Library of Congress Cataloging-in-Publication Data

2005904378

Second Edition

Dedication

This book is dedicated to my daughter,

Melissa Taylor Kelly.

Daddy Loves you!

~ ◆ ~

In Memory of:

Timothy E. Murphy
May 12th, 1891 - February 15th, 1984
The best Grandfather a boy could ever have.

Bruce E. McGrath
June 10th, 1941 - November 20th, 2004
A good man, a great client. We all miss you.

Prologue

Senior Safe Money Strategies(SM) is a collection of my thoughts and a collection of my writings from the last eleven years of working with seniors and their insurance and investments. This book is intended to be an antidote for the poison of fear and greed. That poison is spread by the media.

The first part of the book presents to the reader my thought process concerning investments and is heavily opinionated. Later, estate planning is explored. The last part of the book contains more information and facts than it does opinion. There are some added informational chapters to help seniors in need of advice in areas related to money, investing and any problems that may occur in those areas of their lives.

This book is the result of my work as well as eight years of seminars presented to several thousand seniors. It incorporates most of what I present on a weekly basis over lunch or dinner to those seniors. They are willing to invest their time to see if it may make sense to allow me to assist them in helping them invest their money.

Thus far it has been extremely rewarding for me. If you ask my clients I am hopeful they would tell you it is working extremely well for them also. I am seeking long term growth relationships with clients who need to crystallize and plan for their financial future. They then live into the future as constructed.

How much room is there in your life for a sound financial plan? How much time do you have to devote to planning your financial future? What do you feel such a plan might do for you? How much of your financial future do you want to ad-lib or build on the fly as you go? Probably not much... How much of it do you want to plan for properly and construct ahead of time? Probably most of it.

What we may want to title a book like this is: "How can I be of help to you?" Getting to know each other well enough to have that happen is probably what is required. It requires expert skills and planning. Every carpenter has the same tools; some use them better than others.

Remember, when the house where you live was built, it required an architect, an engineer and an approved set of plans. No construction took place, not a nail was driven until the carpenters were sure everyone had done their jobs in the planning stage. As your home was constructed people who understood the construction process inspected it for soundness. The building of your home is where good planning paid off. Your house has probably provided you with lots of enjoyment as well as reliable shelter over the years. Your home grew in value at a pace greater than the rate of inflation. A good estate plan and investment strategy can provide you with similar peace of mind.

What do my clients want to gain from a relationship with me?

People want to maintain what they have accumulated. They do not want to suffer large losses. Most seek a higher degree of safety or to minimize risk. Some of my clients seek to increase the return on their investments.

Some may want to move an investment from an outdated product into a more modern product. You may want to explore tax advantages. You may want to decrease the amount of worry you have about your retirement choices and increase the fun and enjoyment by planning it out and living it. Some people just want a helping hand consolidating statements and reducing the number of areas where assets are located.

Looking back on it after the process, you may think that having someone there beside you, a financial professional, with appropriate suggestions, answers or solutions was indeed, a good thing.

Some people want to have a sense of greater empowerment. Others want help for a spouse who was previously uninvolved in the planning process. Others want to diversify and take advantage of new legislation in the area of taxes or estate planning. Some people do their entire financial or investment plan with us. Others just come in to check on one or two aspects of their investments.

Looking back, some people find that having met with an estate planning professional whom they trust early on, having worked with that person over the long haul and planning their financial future, has produced a result that is nothing short of remarkable.

Whatever the reason, the more you plan for the long term, the more you seem to benefit and enjoy both the short term and the future as you look back on a sound planning process.

I help people to plan investments, retirement and to do estate planning. I work with ordinary people just like you. Factory workers, aerospace engineers, hair stylists, etc. I work with affluent people and professionals.

I am non proprietary. You may want to know what being "non proprietary" means. One good way to tell if you are with a proprietary firm is to look at the broker's or agent's business card and the title of the policy or product you have purchased and the sign on the building. If all the titles are the same, you are most likely with a proprietary firm.

A proprietary agent might have a more limited universe of product to offer you as you progress through your financial planning process. Sometimes management at proprietary firms has a "stock of the day" or a "product of the month." They might offer agents or brokers immediate rewards or bounties for selling a particular product to you.

Some proprietary firms make markets in certain stocks or make pledges for IPO's or initial public offerings. They then conduct telemarketing campaigns to sell the offerings or to fulfill their pledges to the underwriters. At times a stock broker will be asked to offer new issues to their entire client base regardless of the needs of individuals comprising that base. We do not. —— I think we are different. The only telemarketing I do is to invite people to have dinner at one of my seminars.

We are helping clients work toward financial goals through a wide range of informed choices. I pride myself in service. I am proud of the technology we possess.

My conduct is governed by the compliance standards of the SEC, NASD, and the state insurance commission and banking commission. From time to time my business may be audited by any of those agencies. I take it very seriously.

That being said, these agencies only create a framework of laws, rules and regulations we as professionals must follow. Just being registered or approved does not imply my investment choices are approved. There is no test for investment results I have yet seen. You must be the judge.

What it is all about is a process, not an event; continuing and ongoing management of an estate plan. The plan is fluid and not rigid, as is life. Planning is a marathon and not a quick sprint. Staying power is important.

At some point in time people may decide do business with us. At some point in time after that happens they will become not only a client but may consider us friends. And that usually happens as time passes.

The person you turn to and kiss good-night before drifting off is not your financial advisor (except perhaps if you are my wife....) and it certainly isn't your insurance agent. But we do want you to have a good night's sleep!

I am seeking long term relationships with those who are investing for time periods of five years or more. I am not interested in exact minute by minute timing, although there are some timing aspects in structuring some portfolios or investment plans.

For the most part, the value of time, in my opinion, is more predictable than timing.

You may have estate planning needs. You may have many different IRAs and 401Ks that can be combined into one plan. You may have too much insurance or not enough. You may be paying too much insurance premium for too little face value. Your asset allocation may not actually be what it seems to be.

Investments, retirement and estate planning are what I deal with. Some of you may have differing needs and are at different times and places in your processes. We are all on a path and all in a somewhat unique place on our path.

Your estate is the sum total of all you have on this earth right now. By the way, you are guaranteed to take the sum total of NONE of it with you when you pass from the face of this earth. Retirement is actually provided out of the value of the estate. With proper planning, hopefully there will be enough left over when the estate passes to support a surviving spouse or children if necessary.

Aren't we all hoping to enjoy retirement ? Aren't we guaranteed to pass from this earth? If we knew exactly when these things were going to happen we could plan a little more exactly. I guess the ideal plan would allow us to spend our last dime immediately prior to our last breath. That might not be what we want to do in actuality.

Within your estate you can do only two types of things and two things only: You can do things for yourself or things for others. That's about it! At some point you must decide how and when to do these things. Hopefully the planning process will make these decisions more organized, focused and crystal clear.

You are probably concerned with:
- Defending your investments against unnecessary risk.
- Preserving wealth you have accumulated throughout your retirement years.
- Building more wealth at a pace that exceeds inflation.
- Insuring your wealth.
- Passing on what is left to loved ones or heirs with maximum advantages and minimum taxation.

Strategies and advantages are abundant for you. Think of it as constructing a good defense. You may have had a good offensive strategy. You may have accumulated a substantial amount of wealth, or as my grandfather, Tim Murphy would say, "You have a little something."

You may have hit some financial home runs in your investment process. But most coaches agree that defense wins championships. John Elway, a quarterback, was rated as one of the best offensive players of all time. John Elway went to the Super Bowl three times and lost. Then his team went out and got themselves a first class defense. They won their next two Super Bowls.

Mark McGuire was one of baseballs greatest offensive players. But he sat in the stands and watched the playoffs the year he hit 70 home runs. His team had a poor defense. The Yankees with outstanding defense and pitching and no big home run hitters won the championship that year. Defense wins championships. Great coaches believe defense travels with the team. (Oh, another thing that wins championships is TEAM EFFORT!)

What is financial defense? And what are we defending against? It is risk. You need to defend against risk: Market risk, inflation risk, credit risk, concentration and principal risk are all types of risk. A type of risk that may not have been on the radar screen for Americans as much previously is currency or monetary risk. Terrorism also creates risk to your investments.

My job is to work toward minimizing risk for clients. In the planning process we always include an analysis of risk. After we begin the planning process, at some time folks will be offered solutions. We first address what we consider the most pressing needs and then move on to others in order of importance.

Our clients tend to think of the process to be cafeteria style. In other words, they come and visit with me, see what I have to offer and take what they need from the process. They take advantage of what is attractive to them and leave the rest. These prospects can take what they need and leave the rest on the table. I always respect their choices.

My experience offers me the ability to present you with quality choices. In presenting people with these choices I hope they also feel involved in an educational process. That is not to say all people are in need of education about estate planning. Our clients are very bright; astute for the most part. But I feel that there is always something that a financial professional who works full time at maintaining your portfolio can offer you.

I also learn about and from a client as I work. So it is an educational process for both parties.

If we refer someone to an attorney or an accountant for estate planning or tax consultation we are doing so because we have a great deal of trust in those professional people. We receive no direct benefit except knowing we have referred folks to someone we feel is a high caliber professional. I do try to refer clients to attorneys and accountants who are conscious of keeping costs down and fees low for our referrals.

My approach is to bring Wall Street to Main Street. By fact finding, evaluating, conferencing, calculating ratios and systematizing estate planning we are able to bring services to people in a new way. The basis of my practice is: RESPECT.

William A. Kelly

Table of Contents

I Investment Planning

Senior Safe Money Strategies^{sm}

Some of you reading this book may remember the Great Depression. World War II may not be a distant memory to you. The Marshall Plan followed as we helped to rebuild Europe. You may have lived through the Korean War. You may recall other historical events and programs such as: the Cold War, the Race for Space, the New Frontier, the Great Society, the War on Poverty, Vietnam, the Moon Landing, the Space Shuttle Program, the War on Drugs, the Gulf War and the War in Iraq.

Going through those times what has our government asked of you? Of course money! Not only have you paid taxes, the federal government needed support, votes and old-fashioned American hard work.

So you were paying off the house, repairing that first automobile, raising the kids, paying for tuition and weddings. You were also paying for health care, paying social security taxes and withholding taxes. You were supportive of our government for the most part all along. You were doing what needed to be done to maintain freedom. You enjoyed living in our free nation. In turn you shared in the American dream of a safe place, rich in resources and opportunity. If you liked what the folks in government did, you reelected them. If you got tired of what the politicians said or did, you voted them out.

As a senior, you paid the price all along, whether as a member of the greatest generation or the baby boom generation. And you asked for nothing in return.

Nothing was asked, except for liberty and a place to raise your family and enjoy life and later to pass on that freedom to another generation.

And another thing – all the while you were doing more. You were doing more saving, investing or putting a little something away each day, week or month. That's right, you were doing something extra. I work with seniors, business owners and professionals; people who are at or near retirement. Our clients need help with retirement plans and estate planning. We generally work with affluent people, but that is not a qualifier. I help everyone who comes through our door, who wants and needs my help. If people need my help but cannot afford my services then I feel they are entitled to them at no charge. And I am a top earner, by the way.

I am blessed in many ways. I have the luxury of helping anyone who comes to me and need help. On the other hand, I also have the luxury of telling certain people I just don't want to work with them if I do not feel just right about it.

Over the years, I have developed the program entitled Senior Safe Money Strategies℠. I am quite proud of the program. This program centers on guarantees in writing for the client by the company with whom they invest. I try to locate firms that will guarantee clients returns with no losses of principal due to risk. I try to find products guaranteed by a legislated asset ratio. It means a ratio of cash deposits to the reserves of the investor's assets must be written into law and it must be favorable to the client.

My program is suitable for people willing to accept somewhere in the approximate range of a 3% to 14% return, with a guaranteed minimum return and no risk of principal. The guarantees are often based upon the underlying strength of an issuing insurance company with fixed annuities, of course. But there are laws on the books and regulations in my state, Massachusetts. They describe the investment ratios for the issuing companies. I have a great deal of faith in legislation in this area. If it is written into law, I feel it goes one step further than regulations do.

The "safe" assets are calculated by subtracting the client's age from 90 and moving that smaller percentage amount only, into risk investments. So, if you are 68 years of age, we subtract that from 90 and we come up with 22% of investable assets available to risk. 78% then should be moved to an asset with little or no risk.

These accounts are geared to produce a return even under the worst stock market conditions. They also pass to heirs outside of probate and have liquidity to allow the senior flexibility.

At the end of the day, each and every day, all of our Senior Safe Money Strategies^{SM} clients should expect to have one thing: the same amount at least or hopefully a little more money.

Senior Safe Money Strategies^{SM} clients do not have to read the headlines in the morning wondering if they are going to have a good day or a bad day. They are not scouring the business page wondering if they missed a good value or if their investments are now at the mercy of some courtroom proceeding, misstatement of earnings or regulatory investigation.

These clients are informed of potential risks. They are equipped with choices. They are educated in the purpose of every investment and each action taken in their estate plan.

Senior Safe Money Strategies^{SM} client guaranteed products' values simply remain the same or grow a tiny bit each day, regardless of headlines, cable TV news programs or threats to our nation's security by terrorists. Their risk investments are evaluated each quarter during face to face meetings. Goals are established. Benchmarks are created. Measurement is performed with the client and decisions are made with the client, not for the client.

Senior Safe Money Strategies^{SM} is a process not a transaction. It is an ongoing process involving regular client reviews, consultations with top estate planning attorneys and availability on my part and that of my staff.

How I Learned

How do investment professionals learn what to do? And, in other words, what drives them? For the most part, I feel, investment planning is a sales driven profession. Investment reps strive to have "money under management" and client bases to support them.

I find the information pipeline to be structured so information flows from the wholesalers or representatives of huge investment companies. This flow of ideas or "stories" moves to the headquarters of the brokerage houses to branch offices and then to the individual agents or "reps."

Since we are a free enterprise nation, this also makes for vibrancy in the selling arena. But it often makes for an investment community driven by dependency on sales ideas, not on service, originality or individual broker research. I research constantly, on my own.

I present seminars to seniors at least twenty times a year. The people who attend these dinner workshops and daytime "luncheon learns" are great people. They are searching for knowledge, information and guidance. (We do like to have some fun at the seminars, by the way.) These folks are part of what I consider to be our greatest generation and their children, the baby boom generation. They have worked long and hard and asked little else all of their lives other than: "What can we do to help?"

I entered into the business of estate planning in 1994. It was near the height of the bull market. As I look back it was the beginning of a frenzy. As a former engineer I needed a scientific approach to investing in order to feel right about things. I decided to use Harry Markowitz's theories. Harry won the Nobel Prize in 1990 in economics. He devised modern portfolio theory and the efficient frontier of risk. I decided to adopt his theories.

Harry's theories of the efficient frontier of risk and asset allocation allowed us to judge the amounts of risk we wanted to undertake in order to obtain certain targeted returns. It involved asset classes and rebalancing. Portfolio management, according to Markowitz, was an ongoing series of actions requiring risk management and often, changes in client investments. Now we generally accept that investing within portfolios should be diversified across multiple asset classes. These classes might be stocks and bonds and may also be spread over multiple asset and investment styles. There is plenty of investment information on-line today. Actually it can be overwhelming. It might seem obvious that this Nobel award winning idea would be accepted as a rule of thumb. Believe it or not, it is not as well practiced as one might think. Individual investors can lose out when rational thinking and mathematical calculation are overcome by emotion and "gut feeling."

The classes and styles of investments include growth, value, blends, large cap, mid cap and small cap. There are micro caps, bond and specialty energy, foreign, utility and real estate categories. Aggressive growth, income and capital preservation are considered risk categories for tolerance purposes.

A recent study by Richard Thaler of the Graduate School of Business, University of Chicago found that a significant factor regarding allocating assets in a person's retirement plan was the number and type of choices offered, not the actual substance of the choices. In other words, if there were only two choices in an account, a bond and an equity fund, people tended to split their account evenly between the two. When given more stock funds to choose from, participants tended to move higher percentages into those funds. With more fixed income choices, people tend to utilize them more. Some retirement plans go the other way and offer so many choices that people can become confused.

Remember this: Investors own investments. Investors are NOT investments however. Investments do not have emotions, they are not human. The statistics are real. Sometimes starkly so.

Investor performance does not equal investment performance, unfortunately. Dalbar, Inc., is the nation's leading financial-services market research firm. Examining the flows into and out of mutual funds for the 20 years prior to 2004, the Dalbar study of investor behavior found that market timers in stock mutual funds lost 3.29% per year on average. As for individual investors, over a period when the S&P grew by 12.98% per year the average investor earned only 3.51%. Why? Because investors tend to "buy high and sell low" according to Dalbar. This is especially true when they act on emotions, on their own. As my career began and as the bull market raged on, I noticed a few things:

First, everybody liked what Harry Markowitz had to say. It seemed few people were able to use his findings to directly benefit the clients, according to what I was seeing.

The second thing that seemed unusual to me was how firms seemed to gather assets first and look out for the clients' needs later. I also noticed that client percentages in "safe" money were insufficient in many portfolios, in my opinion. In other words, the market was racing higher every month it seemed, but few people seemed to have cash positions in their portfolios in case there was a sudden downturn. Very few people seemed to be selling. If a portfolio is to be balanced, I thought, why should it have no cash? If the market was reaching record levels, wasn't the possibility of a sharp downturn ever present?

Few people were anticipating a downturn, in my opinion, including planners, clients, market analysts and news pundits. Any media outlet depending on the financial services for advertising support seemed to downplay any warning of the market having "topped out."

In anticipating an eventual downturn, the client assets needed to be positioned in order to take advantage of such an occurrence. In other words, if there was a cash "ballast" in the portfolio, then the client could take advantage of a sharp downturn. They could do so by using that ballast capital to reinvest at lower prices and balancing out the portfolio structure. If there was cash clients could "sit on the sidelines" or dollar cost average on the way up after a sharp market decline.

Back in the early nineties, some people were walking out of the offices unhappy with a projection of potential 12% gains. They were sure they could do better. After all, the broker down the street or up the lane or across town was projecting 18%, 24% or whatever. Just pick a number, any number, because they were all out there in 1994.

Bears win, Bulls win, Pigs are slaughtered

Meanwhile, somewhere in the rear offices of the company, I began studying for my more advanced licenses. At the time I was meeting with some senior clients of the firm from as far back as 1984. These folks all seemed to think alike. They came in with small contracts, often in folders, called fixed annuities. Many of the contracts had matured.

Now here is the most amazing thought process of all that I noticed during the years of raging bull! These people were all satisfied with a guaranteed return; a return of and a return on their investments!

When I asked these long-standing clients how I could help them, they all pretty much said the same thing, "We would like to do this again." Now there was a great difference in these people and those in the securities end of the firm wanting to have returns projected that were "off the chart."

These people were content. They were satisfied and certainly not greedy. The people who had invested into the fixed annuities seemed satisfied with a guaranteed stated return. They had learned to manage their emotions and I think it was working for them. Many or most of them wanted to continue.

No fear and no greed were involved it seemed. People wanted a return on their investment. They wanted a return OF their investment, more importantly! They wanted a general idea of what the risk and return was going to be. And, they wanted very limited principal risk. The bull market raged on. Few people knew it was heading for several disastrous periods. Few knew the mess we were heading for in terms of violations of trust, media manipulation and over inflated valuation. I recalled over and again how these people acted and looked at me. They were content, even in 1994 when they chose to sit out the "bull" market.

Years later, they proved to be right. And, thanks to those people and my interest in what made them seem so satisfied and content I was able to create a practice that could provide peace of mind to my clients and me as well when the wheels finally came off of the runaway wagon called the "raging bull."

Irrational
Exuberance:
December 15, 1996

At the Annual Dinner and Francis Boyer Lecture of The
American Enterprise Institute for Public Policy Research,
Washington, D.C., the Chairman of the Federal Reserve, Alan
Greenspan gave an address. His words included the following:

*"But how do we know when irrational exuberance has unduly
escalated asset values, which then become subject to
unexpected and prolonged contractions as they have in Japan
over the past decade?"*

I can recall December 15, 1996. Many people in the media and the markets chose not to heed the warnings. Those people I met with the folders containing the fixed annuity contracts apparently got the message. Those investments were protected from several market crashes or bottoms still to come. Those contracts were not included in the scandals that shook our industry to the core and the untold market losses of trillions of dollars in value.

Those early meetings signaled the beginnings of my Senior Safe Money Strategy^{SM} program.

Lots of bright people start out in this business with quickness of mind or world burning speed. Many of these people "burn out." Those who steadfastly continue on are the most solid performers.

I like to do my own research. I like to take my time. Clients do a lot of work too! For the most part, firms do not hire representatives and then send them off to an academy somewhere to study portfolio analysis or risk reward scatter plots. They hire new brokers to gather assets. And they were being hired in droves as the market ran up.

A Funny Thing Happened During the Summer of 1998

Sometime in the summer in 1998 the market decided to do something strange. It decided to drop by almost 20% in a period of weeks. Now let's look at what market we are talking about and what happened before and afterward.

From July 20th to August 31st, 1998 The Dow and the NASDAQ index dropped 14% and 18% respectively.

Chairman Greenspan had made his warning speech in December 1996 stating the irrational exuberance of the markets might cause a collapse, but the speech fell on mostly deaf ears. Television personalities were predicting an unending bull market. No one chose to listen, as far as I could determine, to Chairman Greenspan.

If we were to look at the NASDAQ level from September 18th, 1998 until July, 2004, the market shows a net loss over the six year period.

So for those of us unfortunate to have money invested in that market as a whole for that period of time we have had 100% of it at risk for a negative return.

But in the summer of 1998, when the market shuddered, the message was unheeded. For the most part, what happened in the summer of 1998 foretold the future, but few people chose to listen to voices of caution. Caution was thrown to the wind.

The Meaning of ROI:
Return on Investment,
Return of Investment
and Reliability of Income

Now, back to those early clients with the guaranteed fixed annuities. I recalled over and again how these people acted and looked at me. They were content, even in 1994 when they chose to sit out the "bull" market.

Yes there are surrender charges for early withdrawal, and yes the fixed annuity is guaranteed by the underlying issuer's financial strength. But consumers who are savvy enough to locate highly rated ("A" or better) companies with liquidity features built into their annuity may be surprised at the flexibility of modern fixed annuities.

A Pat on the Back

I often tell my clients to make sure they give themselves a "pat on the back" because of the tremendous amount of thought and planning going into what they accomplish by completing an estate plan.

There are only two types of things to do with your wealth, things for yourself and things for someone else. That is about it, plain and simple. For the vast majority of my clients, the choice is to do something for others. They want to keep what they have, grow it a bit and pass it along when they are done. That is admirable.

Further, as they continue to do what they have done all of their lives, something for others, they deserve a lot of credit.

Frankly, if their investable assets increased in value by 50% overnight, it would not change much about the way they lived. But a sudden loss of 30% or more might cause great worry and sleepless nights. Preservation is important. No, it is vital. I have a great deal of respect regarding the time, thought and energy these folks devote to the tasks at hand.

Where are the Client Yachts?

I often wonder why the professionals have the yachts and the clients are always calling them there and not vice versa. We have a rewards based society. I believe the seniors expect their advisors to do well. After all, who wants their planner to live in a shack and hold meetings in hotel lobbies or diners? Sometimes I think some people in the industry carry things a little too far, however.

The seniors do expect their advisors to do well and most of the folks I've met actually want them to do well. Many seniors look at the prosperity of their planners as a symbol that they are "champions." We all know how Americans feel about champions. We like winners.

Money is Money. Risk is not Gambling.

We all use money to purchase investments, but money is not investments! Money is money! Risk is not gambling. Risk is a calculated measure of the possibility of or probability of loss. Threat is not risk but it is a danger to financial security. We need to keep clear in our minds the differences in these: Money, risk, gambling investing. We need to decide as planners and as clients how and how much we want to be exposed.

Senior Safe Money Strategies℠ program clients simply learn to live with the fact that they should have the same thing each day: a little more money. And tomorrow they should have the same thing: a little more money.

Important: Before you invest in any product read all disclosure material provided by an issuing company. If the investment product is a fixed or equity index annuity, then the underlying or issuing financial institution, usually an insurance company, backs it. Research into Best Ratings or Fitch ratings is important. I only utilize companies with ratings of "A" or higher.

Remember: These fixed investments are dependent upon the underlying strength of the guaranteeing institution.

How "Beat the Street" Hurts Seniors.

Some years ago a genius somewhere came up with the idea to sell stocks of companies that had no earnings, were losing some money or losing tons of money. I call this idea the "Beat the Street" scenario.

This scenario can be harmful to investors, but especially so, in my opinion, to seniors. I also call "beat the street" by another name, that is: "putting some lipstick on a piglet to see who kisses it."

How does this happen? Let's say Premier Conglomerated Widget Technologies (PCWT) reports negative earnings of $3.45 a share. Now how does the average senior even know what that means? Say PCWT has ten million shares outstanding. Therefore by losing $3.45 a share then it is losing $34,500,000 dollars in a year's time. That is thirty-four million, five hundred thousand dollars, by the way.

Now how does someone invest in such a company or become interested in doing so? In other words, how does someone put some "lipstick on this piglet?"

It's simple. Someone, somewhere convinces somebody that PCWT is "under priced." If something is under priced, we as Americans may embrace it because we all have the desire to own a bargain. Even if we do not desire to own something initially, it can become more and more attractive to us depending on how much of a "bargain it is."

Well a genius somewhere came up with the scenario of "predicted earnings." Someone, somewhere tells us what to think! In other words a group of people accepted as authorities tells us. You and I have no idea who they are. We do not know their credentials, intent, knowledge or motivation. Together they are collectively called "The Street." Somewhere in the world at some point in time, these people got together and formed a "Street Consensus."

As Americans we are kept busy just running our own lives, keeping things in order and staying current with our own families. Our occupations are all encompassing. Most of us have little time for researching finance or stock portfolios.

We also, as Americans, look to "experts" many times to know what to think or how to think. Recently I saw a Supreme Court decision, the same decision mind you, reported by one source as going against the President and reported by another source as being decided for the President. After a few days everyone settled down and it was widely accepted as being about midway between the two viewpoints. Martha Stewart made hundreds of millions of dollars telling us what to think. Dan Rather and others tell us not just the news, but what to think about the news. We as Americans often do not have time or all the information on hand to form an exact informed opinion. We often rely upon others, the experts, to lead us in our thinking.

Now back to the widgets; How do we make PCWT attractive to investors? Well, let's say the street consensus makes some grand announcement on October 1st that PCWT is projected to post a loss per share of $4.05. It is big news and we are all made aware of it. We may learn it on one of the "after the bell" shows or in the "earnings notes" section of our favorite investment publication. There's more to come, however.

Now, sometime during the following January, there is an equally huge announcement. Some kind of inside scoop or "heard it on the street" preview precedes it.

Somewhere around the end of January we all find out, usually "after hours" to increase the drama that PCWT posts a loss of $3.45 dollars a share instead OF $4.05!

In effect PCWT officially "Beat the Street!" Now this typically excites the "investment community," whoever they are. This great news may cause a buying spree on the next market opening, since this astounding announcement after all came after hours. But the sobering question is: Aren't they still losing a heck of a lot of money? Yes they "Beat the Street" and yes they did better than expected. But aren't we all sort of taking our eyes off of the real issue?

I mean, the company is losing money, lots of it. Someone somewhere has figured out a way to keep the investment respectable, by saying it beat some imaginary figure put out by "The Street."

What does this imaginary panel of people have to lose? Why is losing money a good thing? Is it because we thought PCWT was going to lose a gigantic amount and they ended up losing only a huge amount?

In my mind those were the questions many people failed to ask back in the years 2000 and 2001. Well, the piglet was PCWT company. "Beating the Street," was the lipstick and the people who bought Premier Conglomerated Widget Technologies stock at the opening were "kissing the piglet."

I don't know how to pick up the phone and call whomever the "street" is or to ask someone on the "consensus" committee if losing so much money is good or bad. I do feel there was far too much of this sort of thing going on back in the late 1990's and in the years 2000 and 2001. When everything came crashing down around us though, the "chickens came home to roost" and the piglets kind of ran out of the barnyard, never to be seen or heard from again. Many people had their hopes and dreams invested into this madness. Many seniors had jumped onto the wagon of "beating the street," and other scenarios that proved disastrous, to say the least.

William A. Kelly's Senior Planning Bill of Rights

What each and every client and prospect deserves and should

expect from a professional.

Senior Planning Bill of Rights

The Right To Honesty and Responsible Advice

As a senior, you have a right to fair and honest treatment. You have a right to be informed regarding all aspects of your investments. This may include risk, surrender charges, management fees and more. You have the right to a full disclosure of material facts, obligations and costs.

The Right To Be Informed and the Freedom of Choice, The Right To Privacy and Confidentiality

As a senior, you have the right to know why we need certain information and how it will be used to help you as our client. At Kelly Financial Services we will not disclose any information about you to any others with out your full, prior knowledge and permission.

The Right of Time to Make Decisions

As a senior, you have a right to make an informed decision over a period of time without pressure.

The Right to Suitable Investments

As a senior, you have a right to invest only in products suitable for your age, income and life circumstances.

The Right to Responsiveness, Action and Best Efforts Management

As a senior, you have the right to regular reviews of your investment regardless of the amount of your investment activity or account size. Remember the attention you received as a prospect, You should receive even more as a client, not less.

The Right to Risk Assessment and Explanation of Risks

As a senior, you have the right to know the risks of any investment, to understand them and only undertake those risks if you fully understand them, feel they are suitable and accept them.

The Right of Accountability

As a senior, you have a right to expect accountability from your investment professional. This means regular reviews and establishing goals, benchmarks and milestones.

The Freedom of Flexibility

Plans should be revocable and changeable with maximum flexibility and simplicity.

William Kelly and Kelly Financial Services attempts to achieve the above objectives with each and every client and prospect.

It is important to note that estate planning is a very complex activity. Clients should understand many investments fluctuate in value sometimes causing a contract holder to have more or less money at the day of liquidation. Additionally, the flexibility of an investment can create tax implications and added commission costs. Consult a tax advisor before making changes. Please carefully read all disclosure documents before investing money.

Fear, Hope and Greed: Pushing Buttons is Not Good

Some "marketers" of securities instill or appeal to, one of

three emotions in the clients "investor emotional inventory."

These three emotions are Fear, Hope and Greed.

Fear: If a client is "sold" through fear of loss or fear of missing out on a gain, then that emotion can be used to control the client when markets turn against them. The selling person then knows how to control the client and the account forever by simply referring back to the original point of fear in any subsequent contact with the potentially dissatisfied client. The same goes for hope and greed.

Example of a Fear Based Conversation:

Client: "Gee, Mr. Professional, the portfolio has gone down 20% and you haven't called me or changed any of my positions in my account!"

Fear Based Sales Response: "Mr. Client, if you missed one month of each of the last three bull markets you would have lost almost 50% of the upside of those markets, is that what you want or should we wait it out?"

Example of a Hope Based Conversation:

Client: "Gee, the portfolio has gone down 20% and you haven't called me or changed any of my positions in my account!"

Hope Based Sales Response: "Mr. Client, we said we would hope for a 12% gain, and if you look at the S&P over the last twenty five years, that's what has occurred. Can you find a better investment? Let's wait it out.

Example of a Greed Based Conversation:

Client: "Gee, the portfolio has gone down 20% and you haven't called me or changed any of my positions in my account!"

Greed Based Response: "Mrs. Client, we are in this for the big money, we really should be shorting the market or using margin, but I don't think you have the stomach for it. As you know I place your interests above even my own. My daughter holds these same securities. My clients who are shorting are making a killing today. These positions we now have are where the future lies. As you know, vision has its price but the people who are there first and pay the price always get the top rewards."

My clients and I never have to engage in these conversations. They have made a decision beforehand as to what an acceptable minimum gain is satisfactory. They want to keep what they have, grow it a little after inflation and taxes and pass on what is left.

At the end of the day, each and every day they have the same results after inflation and taxes are overcome. They generally can expect to have a little more money. First and foremost, we have to decide, with the client what a reasonable rate of return is. The clients must manage their expectations and we must manage their cases. When a conversation similar to those cited above takes place then the representative is no longer managing assets, in my opinion, they are managing peoples' emotions. At that point the client could be at the mercy of the rep's psychological and sales skills rather than asset management skills.

Our clients do not have to read the headlines and wonder if they're going to have a good day investment wise. If there is risk then we inform them about the type and nature before hand. We like to try and minimize risk and then try to maximize return.

The Six T's

Threats to Senior Investors and how to overcome them.

The First "T" – Time

What do young people have lots of that seniors have little of? Time of course. But, seniors seem to have the assets while youngsters are still in the accumulation mode. Lack of time horizons may prohibit risk. Lack of a long horizon may prohibit dollar cost averaging and it may prevent recovery from catastrophic market crashes. Time should not be wasted wondering if decisions are correct. Time, in retirement should be spent enjoying life with those we love.

The Second "T" – Trust Violations

Seniors place a good deal of trust into institutions. When we were kids on the farm sometimes we would visit the bank on Friday evenings. My dad would pile us into the station wagon and off we would go. Sometimes there were seven kids in that station wagon. We would all be dressed neatly, clean and shiny, to go to the bank.

My dad would meet with the banker as we sat on the parson's bench in the bank. We would watch them end the meeting , usually with a handshake in the lobby. Then we would all pile back into the station wagon and head to the local diner for fish and chips. The handshake indicated trust. My dad trusted the banker to follow through on his promises and to provide the best interest rate or service. The banker trusted that my dad would keep his word also. Trust was important.

Those of my Dad's generation began to automatically convey trust to institutions as time passed. Unfortunately, during the years 2000 to 2002 we found some of the names we trusted were actually not worthy of that trust.

The Third "T" – Technology

The markets once became overpriced due to the overvaluation of the technology and internet sector. That led to a market meltdown or crash in 2001.

Technology allows grandparents to "instant message" their grandchildren. It allows us to have same day digital photos of ballet recitals or trips. But, the technology sector may be the last place to put the investments of a retired senior on a budget relying upon the income from a portfolio.

In other words, enjoy the advantages of technology, but beware of investing retirement money into aggressive stocks of unproven or uneven performers.

The Fourth "T" – Taxation

Since 1983, some of the largest tax increases in our nation have occurred for those ages 62 and over. This is due in part to their social security being taxed at an increasingly higher rate. President Roosevelt promised when he signed the Social Security bill in 1936 that they would "never tax social security benefits during my lifetime!" Unfortunately he passed away.

The Estate Tax is the "Grand Daddy" of all taxes. Avoiding or reducing taxation is important!

The Fifth "T" – Television

Television: Sponsored financial broadcasts tend to tout securities. The message is, "BUY! BUY! BUY!" There is seldom a message to sell. For people over 60, I think avoiding a loss is more important than risking all to make a gain.

The Sixth "T" – Terrorism

Terrorism is capable of rattling, paralyzing, shutting down or crashing the market. It has created a single crash followed by unprecedented volatility, in 2001. Unfortunately the threat of terrorism is here to stay. Try to insure your retirement.

The Five A's:
Make a great
report card

There are five "A's" I feel can possibly offset the threats of Time, misuse of Trust, volatile Technology, Taxation, bad information from Television and Terrorist threats.

The First "A" – Attitude

The first is Attitude. My attitude is this: A dollar is a dollar. Let's put it somewhere where someone else agrees with that theory, not somewhere we have to guess about it every day. That is very simple to me. It is definitely an old fashioned notion and one in which I believe.

The New York Stock Exchange is an auction system. Stocks are constantly being auctioned off, bought and sold by the millions of shares each and every day. If you are invested in stocks on that exchange you have to wait and see their "new price" each day. At the end of the day trading stops and all buys and sells end. You then find out what your dollar of stock that morning is worth at four o'clock that afternoon. And that price will usually hold for eighteen hours or so until the market opens and the auction begins all over again.

If the market goes down one hundred and eighty points, your dollar may be worth 96 cents at the end of the day. For the most part, someone else determines the worth of your money each day you have it in stocks and there are no guarantees.

You may have held shares of Exxon for twenty years. Then those temporary daily fluctuations, and even market crashes such as in 1987, 2001 and on September 11th might not affect your psyche too much. However, if you have just invested your entire 401(k) or IRA into growth or technology stocks dependent upon market performance, then those crashes and downturns could spoil your retirement.

Keeping the gains means selling at some time. The message from Wall Street always seems to be BUY, BUY, and BUY! But billionaire Bernard Baruch once said, "I made all of my money by selling a little too soon." Who is there to tell you to sell and go to safety?

The Second "A" – Ability

All mechanics have access to the same tools of the trade, as do carpenters. All surgeons pretty much have the same sets of scalpels and clamps. It is what the professionals do with their tools that make their services so valuable. On the other hand if they are not skillful or prudent, their services can be either valueless or perhaps even harmful.

In the estate planning and investment field we all have pretty much the same tools. We all have thousands of products to select. There are Morningstar™ reports There are rating services like Fitch or A.M. Best or Weiss. I use BigCharts.com for historical and up-to-the-minute quotes. I use Data Island on the web to see the pre-market activity, which begins at 6:55 AM. I use Blomberg to track the Asian markets, which open up on Sunday evening at 7:00 PM eastern time. There is the Internal Revenue Code. There are laws and changes in legislation we all need to study and use to our clients' advantage. Everyone has the same set of research tools, regulations and guidelines. Some of us choose to employ them differently. I may study them and interpret them in a specialized way others do not.

I like to do my own research and then find companies suited to the clients' needs rather than waiting for a salesperson or wholesaler to show up and give me the latest twist on the market or a new story to tell my client.

If I do my own research and afterwards call on a company I have selected, then it creates a different dynamic. I know in advance the rating of the company, the capital structure and the past performance. There are no lingering doubts about having to use their products. I do not have to rely upon the salespeople to convince me to tell their "story" in order to have clients "buy."

Oh, and here is another surprise, I never sell products. I inform clients. They then make the product selection that they feel fits their criteria.

And lastly while we are on the subject of ability, I have the greatest faith in the judgment of my clients. They invest a lot of time with my staff and me.

They have accumulated their wealth, whatever the sum and they come to see me perhaps to do some things for themselves, but 99.9% of my seniors are present to do something for someone else. The "someone else" may mean each other first, then children, grandchildren, nieces or nephews.

They have accumulated these assets, after all of the wars and taxes and sacrifice. I have some ideas about how to protect the downside, minimize risk or manage the assets. I feel I owe it to them to share my knowledge. If I can teach them a little bit and learn about them a lot, we can both travel down a path together. They do not deserve to be either pushed or dragged down the path. The seniors I meet with are capable of understanding the "W's." (The Five W's are outlined in the next chapter).

The Third "A" is Availability

I try to return all calls received before noon on the same day and those after noon during the next business day. If I am out of the office for an extended period, I give clients my cell phone number if need be. If you cannot readily contact your representative then either they have too many clients, are inconsiderate or they are not interested enough in your well being to make contact. It usually is not a good sign.

The Fourth "A" is Action

Measure twice, cut once! Getting things done in itself is daunting at times. We have seminars. It involves inviting the guests, setting up the facility, confirming the guests, seating them and making sure the dinner workshops and daytime luncheon learns are just right. Then we teach certain things at the seminar which I hope give the seniors some knowledge and tools to enable and empower them.

I actually teach at the seminar. I feel that information is important to my guests and clients. Another rule at the seminars is: All are welcome, especially clients. The rule at my Mother's table back on our farm was there was always room for one more person. The same is true of our seminars. If someone is there because they only want to enjoy a night out, then that is fine with our staff and me. Past attendees are welcome as are old and new clients alike.

We have elder law and real estate attorneys with whom we affiliate. The rule in selecting these attorneys is that they are available and that they take action for the clients, when requested to do so.

We analyze each case and illustrate risk and present folks with a balance sheet for estate planning purposes.

We ask the prospects lots of questions and then we process their own answers into a fact find report. I then hand the analysis and report back with some suggestions.

Sometimes we spot something of importance needing immediate attention. We try to help folks tie up loose ends and we encourage them to do their legal work at a fairly fast pace.

The Fifth "A" is Accountability

At the end of the day, when I close the door to the office and look at the sign, my name is on the door. There is a lot of meaning in that for me. I am accountable for all of what happens both at the seminars and within that office suite. This means I have to be there for the clients and do the next right thing each moment and all day long. There are lots of compliance issues, rules and regulations and commissions and governing bodies overseeing my work. We have never had one complaint from a client or prospect, either written or verbal, to any of these overseeing bodies. When all is said and done, we need to be able to do the managing.

The Five W's: Things you need to know about your investments.

Some questions you may want to ask yourself, your spouse or your advisor follow. And I want you to know, you should never feel shy about asking these questions. Actually, as a senior, you need to ask more questions. From my experience, seniors do not speak up enough.

The First "W" is Why

The first question you need to ask about you investments is: Why? Why are you doing what you are doing? Is your goal long term retirement security, are you hoping to grow money rapidly, beat CDs or simply preserve wealth to pass on to your children? Why did your planner choose certain investments in your account? Do they meet the criteria you've set?

The Second "W" is Where

Another important question is: Where? Where is the money? There was a famous TV commercial in the 1980's where a lady asked the famous question about her hamburger, "Where's the beef?" You should be just as vocal and persistent. Knowing and understanding the location and custody of your funds is something that is of paramount importance to you as an investor and especially so for seniors. Is it insured through SIPIC or FDIC? Where do you have to go or to call to get your money when you retire or complete the investment process? Where do your statements come from? Do they come from your advisor or broker or are they produced by a holding company or clearing center? Are you able to call the company where the funds are held and receive interim reports, independent of your advisor?

The Third "W" is When

The next question is: When? When does your investment mature? If it is ongoing, then, when do you need to rebalance? When do you buy more? When should you sell some of the investment? Remember, when to sell is as important as when you should buy an investment. When are surrender charges retired? When do you pay any fees due and how much are they? When do you have reviews? Quarterly? Yearly? Semiannually? When can you take income? When is your MRD (mandatory IRA withdrawal) due and how much?

The Fourth "W" is What?

A very important question is: What is the reason you own an investment, CD, insurance contract, annuity, stock or bond? What for? Also what is the purpose of the intended result of each investment? If you own an insurance policy to create cash for your children should you pass, then the death benefit may be more important than the cash value. If the proceeds of an annuity are never to be used, but you intend to pass it on to a grandchild, then it may allow more risk and a potential higher return. Do you own a mutual fund or a collection of them in a variable annuity? Basically ask yourself and then your planner, "What is the purpose of my investment, what is it supposed to do for me or my loved ones and what are the features, benefits and limitations of this strategy?"

The Fifth "W" is Who?

Lastly, who is managing your investment and how sound is that person or institution? Who will benefit by your investment? You, your spouse or a child or loved one? Who is responsible for performance? Is it market driven or are there guarantees? Who will contact you if there is a problem or a change is needed? Who do you contact for information, changes or rebalancing? Who is the custodian of your funds? Who is the person taking final responsibility for assisting you with your investments and selecting and monitoring them? Does the investment company switch representatives on you frequently? If so then you need to find out the reason.

Estate Planning

Wills

Estate Planning for Everyone

Living Trusts

Wills

Wills are the most common way for people to state their preferences about how their estates should be handled after their deaths. Many people use their wills to express their deepest sentiments toward their loved ones. A well-written will eases the transition for survivors by transferring property quickly and avoiding many tax burdens. Despite these advantages, many estimates figure that at least seventy percent of Americans do not have valid wills. While it is difficult to contemplate mortality, many people find that great peace of mind results from putting their affairs in order.

Wills vary from extremely simple single-page documents to elaborate volumes, depending on the estate size and preferences of the person making the will (the "testator"). Wills describe the estate, the people who will receive specific property (the "devisees"), and even special instructions about care of minor children, gifts to charity, and formation of posthumous trusts. Many people choose to disinherit people who might usually be expected to receive property. For all these examples, the testator must follow the legal rules for wills in order to make the document effective.

Will Requirements

Formal requirements for wills vary from state to state. Generally, the testator must be an adult of "sound mind," meaning that the testator must be able to understand the full meaning of the document. Wills must be written. Some states allow a will to be in the testators own handwriting, but a better and more enforceable option is to use a typed or pre-printed document. A testator must sign his or her own will, unless he or she is unable to do so, in which case the testator must direct another person to sign the will in the presence of witnesses, and the signature must be witnessed and/or notarized. A valid will remains in force until revoked or superseded by a subsequent valid will. Some changes may be made by amendment (called a "codicil") without requiring a complete rewrite.

Will Limitations

Some legal restrictions prevent a testator from giving full effect to his or her wishes. Some laws prohibit disinheritance of spouses or dependent children. A married person cannot completely disinherit a spouse without the spouse's consent, usually in a pre-nuptial agreement. In most jurisdictions, a surviving spouse has a right of election, which allows the spouse to take a legally-determined percentage (up to one-half) of the estate when he or she is dissatisfied with the will. Non-dependent children may be disinherited, but this preference should be clearly stated in the will in order to avoid confusion and possible legal challenges.

Some property may not descend by will. Property owned in joint tenancy may only go to the surviving joint tenant. Also, pensions, bank accounts, insurance policies and similar contracts that name a beneficiary must go to the named party.

Appointing a Representative

A will usually appoints a personal representative (or "executor") to perform the specific wishes of the testator after he or she passes on. The personal representative need not be a relative, although testators typically choose a family member or close friend, as well as an alternate choice. The chosen representative should be advised of his or her responsibilities before the testator dies, in order to ensure that he or she is willing to undertake these duties. The personal representative consolidates and manages the testators assets, collects any debts owed to the testator at death, sells property necessary to pay estate taxes or expenses, and files all necessary court and tax documents for the estate.

Choosing a Guardian

Testators who have minor or dependent children may use a will to name a guardian to care for their children if there is no surviving parent to do so. If a will does not name a guardian, a court may appoint someone who is not necessarily the person whom the testator would have chosen. Again, a testator usually chooses a family member or friend to perform this function, and often names an alternate. Potential guardians should know they have been chosen, and should fully understand what may be required of them. The choice of guardian often affects other will provisions, because the testator may want to provide financial support to the guardian in raising surviving children.

When No Valid Will Exists

If a person dies without a valid will and did not make alternative arrangements to distribute property, survivors may face a complicated, time-consuming, and expensive legal process. Dying without a will leaves an estate "intestate," and a probate court must step in to divide up the estate using legal defaults that give property to surviving relatives. The court pays any unpaid debts and death expenses first, then follows the legal guidelines. The rules vary depending on whether the deceased was married and had children, and whether the spouse and children are alive. If the intestate individual has no surviving spouse, children, or grandchildren, the estate is divided between various other relatives. Therefore, intestacy may mean that people who would never have been chosen to receive property will in fact be entitled to a portion of the estate. Additionally, state intestacy laws only recognize relatives, so close friends or charities that the deceased favored do not receive anything. If no relatives are found, the estate typically goes to the state or local government. Intestacy also poses a heavy tax burden on estate assets. When made aware of the consequences of intestacy, most people prefer to leave instructions rather than subject their survivors and property to government-mandated division.

Estate Planning
for Everyone

Estate planning may ease the distribution of your assets

according to your wishes after your death. Successful estate

planning should flawlessly transfer your assets to your

beneficiaries quickly and with minimal tax consequences. The

process of estate planning includes the inventory of your

assets and making a will and/or establishing a trust, often

with an emphasis on minimizing taxes. This chapter provides

only a general overview of estate planning. You should consult

an attorney, a CPA or tax advisor for additional guidance.

Taking Stock

The first step in estate planning is to inventory everything you own and assign a value to each asset. Here's a list to get you started. You may need to delete some categories or add others.

- Residence

- Other real estate

- Savings (bank accounts, CDs, money markets)

- Investments (stocks, bonds, mutual funds)

- 401(k), IRA, pension and other retirement accounts

- Life insurance policies and annuities

- Ownership interest in a business

- Motor vehicles (cars, boats, planes)

- Jewelry

- Collectibles

- Other personal property

Once you've estimated the value of your estate, you're ready to do some planning. Keep in mind that estate planning is not a one-time job. There are a number of changes that may call for a review of your plan. Take a fresh look at your estate plan if:

- The value of your assets changes significantly.

- You marry, divorce or remarry.

- You have a child.

- You move to a different state.

- The executor of your will or the administrator of your trust dies or becomes incapacitated, or your relationship with that person changes significantly.

- One of your heirs dies or has a permanent change in health.

- The laws affecting your estate change.

How Estates Are Taxed

Federal gift and estate tax law permits each taxpayer to transfer a certain amount of assets free from tax during his or her lifetime or at death. (In addition, as discussed in the next section, certain gifts valued at $11,000 or less can be made that are not counted against this amount.) The amount of money that can be shielded from federal estate or gift taxes is determined by the federal applicable credit. The credit is used during your lifetime when you make certain taxable gifts, and the balance, if any, can be used by your estate after your death.

Keep in mind that while you can plan to minimize taxes, your estate may still have to pay some federal estate taxes. What's more, your estate may be subject to state estate or inheritance taxes, which are beyond the scope of this book. An estate planning professional can provide more information regarding state taxes.

Minimizing Estate Taxation

There are a number of estate planning methods that can be used to minimize federal taxes on your estate.

One of them is giving away assets during your lifetime. Federal tax law generally allows each individual to give up to $11,000* per year to anyone without paying gift taxes, subject to certain restrictions. That means you can transfer some of your wealth to your children or others during your lifetime to reduce your taxable estate. For example, you could give $11,000 a year to each of your children, and your spouse could do likewise (for a total of $22,000 per year to each child). You may make $11,000 annual gifts to as many people as you wish. You may also give your child or another person more than $11,000 a year without having to pay federal gift taxes, but the excess amount will count against the amount shielded from tax by your applicable credit. For example, if you gave your favorite niece $33,000 a year for the last three years, you would have reduced your applicable credit by $66,000 (a $22,000 excess gift each year).

The annual gift tax exclusion will be adjusted for inflation, as measured by the Consumer Price Index (CPI) published by the Department of Labor. The increases will be in multiples of $1,000. This exclusion applies only to a gift of a present interest in property. Therefore, gifts made intrust generally will not qualify for this exclusion.

The marital deduction shields property transferred to a spouse from taxes. Federal tax laws generally permit you to transfer assets to your spouse without incurring gift or estate taxes, regardless of the amount. This is not, however, without its drawbacks. Marital deductions may increase the total combined federal estate tax liability of the spouses upon the subsequent death of the surviving spouse. To avoid this problem, many couples choose to establish a bypass trust.

Bypass trusts or credit shelter trusts can give a couple the advantages of the marital deduction while utilizing the unified credit to its fullest. Let's say, for example, that a married couple has a federal taxable estate worth $2 million (or $1,000,000 each). Using the marital deduction, if one spouse dies in 2003 the full $1,000,000 can be left to the other spouse without incurring taxes. However, when the second spouse dies in 2004 and passes his or her $2 million estate on to their children, taxes will be levied on the excess over the amount of assets shielded by the applicable credit ($2,000,000 - $1,500,000 = $500,000 subject to estate tax).

With a bypass or credit shelter trust, the first spouse to die can leave the amount shielded by the applicable credit to the trust. The trust can provide income to the surviving spouse for life, then upon the death of the surviving spouse the assets are distributed to beneficiaries, such as children. This permits the spouse who dies first to fully utilize his or her applicable credit. If the trust document is drawn properly, the assets in the trust are not included in the surviving spouse's estate. Thus, the surviving spouse's estate will be smaller and can also utilize the applicable credit. In the example above, the surviving spouse's estate would not have to pay federal estate taxes. Because both partners have made use of their applicable credit, the couple is able to pass on a substantial estate tax free to their beneficiaries.

Charitable gifts are not taxed as long as the contribution is made to an organization that operates for religious, charitable or educational purposes. Check to see if the organization you want to give money to is an eligible charity in the eyes of the Internal Revenue Service. You, or your estate may be entitled to a tax deduction for contributions to a qualifying charity. Consult your tax advisor.

Life insurance trusts can be designed to keep the proceeds of a life insurance policy out of your estate and give your estate the liquidity it needs. Generally, you can fund a life insurance trust either by transferring an existing life insurance policy or by having the trust purchase a new policy.* To avoid inclusion in your estate, such trusts must be irrevocable—meaning that you cannot dissolve the trust or change the terms of the trust if you change your mind later. With proper planning, the proceeds from life insurance held by the trust may pass to trust beneficiaries without income or estate taxes. This gives them cash which may be used to help pay estate taxes or other expenses, such as debts or funeral costs.

Estate planning is very complex and is subject to changing laws. This book by no means covers all estate planning methods. Be sure to seek professional advice from a qualified attorney, and perhaps a CPA or estate planner. The money you spend now to plan your estate can mean more money for your beneficiaries in the future.

*Transferring an existing policy may have gift tax consequences. Consult your tax advisor.

Estate Planning Steps
- Make a will. In a will, you state who you want to inherit your property and name a guardian to care for your young children should something happen to you and the other parent.

- Consider a trust. If you hold your property in a living trust, your survivors won't have to go through probate court, a time-consuming and expensive process.

- Make health care directives. Writing out your wishes for health care can protect you if you become unable to make medical decisions for yourself. Health care directives include a health care declaration ("living will") and a power of attorney for health care, which gives someone you choose the power to make decisions if you can't. (In some states, these documents are combined into one, called an advance healthcare directive.)

- Make a financial power of attorney. With a durable power of attorney for finances, you can give a trusted person authority to handle your finances and property if you become incapacitated and unable to handle your own affairs.

Should I be Concerned?

You may think estate planning is only for the wealthy. If your assets are worth $1,000,000 or more, estate planning may benefit your heirs. That's because generally taxable estates worth in excess of the amounts in the chart below may be subject to federal estate taxes, with rates as high as 45% to 50% of the taxable estate.

Adding up the value of your assets can be an eye-opening experience. By the time you account for your home, investments, retirement savings and life insurance policies you own, you may find your estate in the taxable category.

Even if your estate is not likely to be subject to federal estate taxes, estate planning may be necessary to be sure your intentions for disposition of your assets are carried out.

Year	Exclusion Amount	Highest Estate Tax Rate
2002	$1,000,000	50%
2003	$1,500,000	49%
2004	$1,500,000	48%
2005	$2,000,000	47%
2006	$2,000,000	46%
2007	$2,000,000	45%
2008	$2,000,000	45%
2009	$3,500,000	45%

It is also important to note that estate taxes are scheduled to be repealed in 2010. However, if Congress does not affirmatively extend the repeal, in 2011 the estate tax law will revert to the provisions in effect in 2001 including a $1,000,000 exclusion amount and a 55% highest estate tax rate.

The person you name to handle your finances is called your agent or attorney-in-fact (but doesn't have to be an attorney).

Protect your children's property. You should name an adult to manage any money and property your minor children may inherit from you. This can be the same person as the personal guardian you name in your will.

- File beneficiary forms. Naming a beneficiary for bank accounts and retirement plans makes the account automatically "payable on death" to your beneficiary and allows the funds to skip the probate process. Likewise, in almost all states, you can register your stocks, bonds, or brokerage accounts to transfer to your beneficiary upon your death.

- Consider life insurance. If you have young children, own a house, or you may owe significant debts or estate taxes when you die; life insurance may be a good idea.

- Understand estate taxes. If you and your spouse together own assets worth at least $1.5 million, you may want to consider taking steps to reduce federal estate tax that will be due at the second spouse's death. You may want to make tax-free gifts now or consider an AB trust.

- Cover funeral expenses. Rather than a funeral prepayment plan, which may be unreliable, you can set up a payable-on-death account at your bank and deposit funds into it to pay for your funeral and related expenses.

- Make final arrangements. Make your wishes known regarding organ and body donation and disposition of your body -- burial or cremation.

- Protect your business. If you're the sole owner of a business, you should have a succession plan. If you own a business with others, you should have a buyout agreement.

- Store your documents. Your attorney-in-fact and/or your executor (the person you choose in your will to administer your property after you die) may need access to the following documents:

- *Wills and Trusts*

- *Insurance Policies*

- *Real Estate Deeds*

- *Certificates for stocks, bonds, annuities*

- *Information on Bank Accounts, Mutual Funds, and Safe Deposit Boxes*

- *Information on Retirement Plans, 401(k) Accounts, or IRAs*

- *Information on Debts, Mortgages and Loans, Credit Cards, Utilities, and Unpaid Taxes*

- *Information on Totten Trusts or Funeral Pre-payment Plans, and any final arrangements you have made.*

When estate tax is due, who pays? You have been chosen as an executor of someone's will. Here's how to get the answers and the help you need.

What is an executor?

The executor (called a personal representative in some states) is the person named in a will to be in charge of winding up the person's financial affairs after death. Basically, that means taking care of property, paying bills and taxes, and seeing to it that assets are transferred to their new rightful owners. If probate court proceedings are required, as they often are, the executor must handle them or hire a lawyer to do so.

Does the person named in a will as executor have to serve?

No. When it comes time, an executor can accept or decline this responsibility. And someone who agrees to serve can resign at any time. That's why you should name an alternate executor in your will -- a person who can take over from the executor if necessary. If no one is available, the court will appoint someone to step in.

Does an executor get paid?

The main reason most people serve as an executor is to honor the deceased person's request. But the executor is also entitled to payment. The exact amount is regulated by state law and is affected by factors such as the value of the deceased person's property and what the probate court decides is reasonable under the circumstances. Commonly, close relatives and close friends (especially those who are inheriting a substantial amount anyway) don't charge the estate for their services.

Must an executor hire a lawyer?

Not always. Doing a good job requires persistence and attention to tedious detail, but not necessarily a law degree. Shepherding a case through probate court requires shuffling a lot of papers. In the vast majority of cases, there are no disputes that require a decision by a judge and the executor may never see the inside of a courtroom. It may even be possible to do everything by mail.

An executor should definitely consider handling the paperwork without a lawyer if he or she is the main beneficiary, the deceased person's property consists of common kinds of assets (house, bank accounts, insurance), the will seems straightforward, and good self-help materials are at hand.

If, however, the estate has many types of property, significant tax liability or potential disputes among inheritors, an executor may want some help.

There are two ways for an executor to get help from a lawyer:

- Hire a lawyer to act as a "coach," answering legal questions as they come up. The lawyer might also do some research, look over documents before the executor files them, or prepare an estate tax return.

- Turn the probate over to the lawyer. If the executor just doesn't want to deal with the probate process, a lawyer can do everything. The lawyer will be paid out of the estate. In most states, lawyers charge by the hour ($150-$200 is common) or charge a lump sum. But in a few places, including Arkansas, California, Delaware, Hawaii, Iowa, Missouri, Montana, and Wyoming, state law authorizes the lawyer to take a certain percentage of the gross value of the deceased person's estate unless the executor makes a written agreement calling for less. An executor can probably find a competent lawyer who will agree to a lower fee.

Can an executor get help from someone besides a lawyer?

Yes. Here are some other sources of information and assistance.

- The court. Probate court clerks commonly answer basic questions about court procedure, but they staunchly avoid saying anything that could possibly be construed as "legal advice." Some courts, however, have lawyers on staff who look over probate documents, point out errors in the papers, and explain how to fix them.

- Other professionals. For certain tasks, an executor may be better off hiring an accountant or appraiser than a lawyer. For example, a CPA may be a big help on estate tax matters.

- Paralegals. Many lawyers delegate probate paperwork to paralegals. Now, in some areas of the country, experienced paralegals have set up shop to help people directly with probate paperwork. These paralegals don't offer legal advice; they just prepare documents as the executor instructs them, and file them with the court. To find a probate paralegal, an executor can look online or in the Yellow Pages under "Legal Document Preparation" or "Attorney Services." The executor should hire someone only if that person has substantial experience in this field and provides good references.

Definitions

Will:

A will is a written document that takes effect at the death of the person signing it (the "testator"). A will covers all property owned by the testator at death. A state court proceeding ("probate") is instituted and the provisions of the will are implemented under supervision of the probate court. Both the tax and family estate planning objectives of the decedent can be accomplished with a will.

Living Trust:

A living trust (sometimes called an "inter-vivos" trust) is a document that is revocable at any time by the person signing it ("grantor"). Living trusts have become quite popular as a method to avoid probate. To avoid probate, the trust must be funded; this means that title to the assets which the grantor owns personally must be actually transferred to the trust -- real property is deeded to the trust; bank accounts are switched to the trust; and stocks, bonds, partnership interests and other holdings are assigned or transferred to the trust. (Note: The grantor is usually the trustee and beneficiary of the trust during his or her lifetime.)

Use of a Will vs. a Living Trust

Generally, with either a will or a trust the same estate tax consequences occur, and the same opportunities for tax and family planning are available. The debate over the value of each often centers around the savings of the costs incurred in a probate proceeding which typically run between 2 to 4 percent of the value of the probate estate. While a living trust which is fully funded with the grantor's assets prior to his or her death will eliminate probate, there may be advantages to probate which are also lost. In addition, the initial cost and maintenance of the living trust must be considered.

A realistic assessment of the net savings in using a living trust would be approximately 1 to 2 percent of the gross estate; an estate of $1,000,000 should save between $10,000 and $20,000 by using a living trust instead of a will.

The savings must be counter-balanced by the administrative burden of maintaining the assets in the trust over the period of one's life. There are other, non-economic advantages for using a trust which merit consideration such as privacy (a trust is not probated in open court) and upon the incapacity or death of the grantor, the trust continues to operate without court intervention.

Living Trust Offers:

How to Make Sure They're Trustworthy.

You've worked hard for your money, and made every attempt to be a conscientious saver. So it's only natural that you want some control over what happens to your assets in the event of your death. At the very least, you probably want to minimize or avoid potential hassles and headaches for your loved ones.

Estate planning deals with what happens to your assets after you die. Even if you are a person of modest means, you have an estate — and several strategies to choose from to make sure that your assets are distributed as you wish and in a timely way. The right strategies depend on your individual circumstances. That is, what is best for your neighbor might not make the most sense for you.

Make a Trust

- *Decide if you need a shared trust.*

- *Decide what items to leave in the trust.*

- *Decide who will inherit your trust property.*

- *Choose someone to be your successor trustee.*

- *Choose someone to manage children's property.*

- *Prepare the trust and sign it in front of a notary.*

- *Transfer title of property to yourself as trustee.*

- *Store your trust document safely.*

Misinformation and misunderstanding about estate taxes and the length or complexity of probate provide the perfect cover for scam artists who have created an industry out of older people's fears that their estates could be eaten up by costs or that the distribution of their assets could be delayed for years. Some unscrupulous businesses are advertising seminars on living trusts or sending postcards inviting consumers to call for in-home appointments to learn whether a living trust is right for them. In these cases, it's not uncommon for the salesperson to exaggerate the benefits or the appropriateness of the living trust and claim — falsely — that locally-licensed lawyers will prepare the documents.

Other businesses are advertising living trust "kits": consumers send money for these do-it-yourself products, but receive nothing in return. Still other businesses are using estate planning services to gain access to consumers' financial information and to sell them other financial products, such as insurance annuities.

What's a consumer to do? It's true that for some people, a living trust can be a useful and practical tool. But for others, it can be a waste of money and time. What is a living trust, anyway, and how does it differ from a will? Who should you trust when it comes to estate planning? And how can you tell which tools and strategies will work best for your particular circumstances?

The Federal Trade Commission, the government agency that works to prevent fraud, deception and unfair business practices in the marketplace, says that it helps to learn the terms that are used in this aspect of financial planning before you begin conversations about it. For example:

Probate is a legal process that usually involves filing a deceased person's will with the local probate court, taking an inventory and getting appraisals of the deceased's property, paying all legal debts, and eventually distributing the remaining assets and property. This process can be costly and time-consuming. Many states have simplified probate for estates below a certain amount, but that amount varies among states. If an estate meets the state's requirements for "expedited" or "unsupervised" probate, the process is faster and less costly.

A *trust* is a legal arrangement where one person (the "grantor") gives control of his property to a trust, which is administered by a "trustee" for the "beneficiary's" benefit. The grantor, trustee and beneficiary may be the same person. The grantor names a successor trustee in the event of incapacitation or death, as well as successor beneficiaries.

A *living trust*, created while you're alive, lets you control the distribution of your estate. You transfer ownership of your property and your assets into the trust. You can serve as the trustee or you can select a person or an institution to be the trustee. If you're the trustee, you will have to name a successor trustee to distribute the assets at your death.

The advantage of a living trust? Properly drafted and executed, it can avoid probate because the trust owns the assets, not the deceased. Only property in the deceased's name must go through probate. The downside? Poorly drawn or unfunded trusts can cost you money and endanger your best intentions.

A *will* is a legal document that dictates how to distribute your property after your death. If you don't have a will, you die intestate. The laws of your state will determine what happens to your estate and your minor children. The probate court governs this process.

A living trust is different from a living will. A living will expresses your wishes about being kept alive if you're terminally ill or seriously injured.

And, the FTC advises, proceed with caution. Because state laws and requirements vary, "cookie-cutter" approaches to estate planning aren't always the most efficient way to handle your affairs. Before you sign any papers to create a will, a living trust, or any other kind of trust:

- Explore all your options with an experienced and licensed estate planning attorney or financial advisor. Generally, state law requires that an attorney draft the trust.

- Avoid high-pressure sales tactics and high-speed sales pitches by anyone who is selling estate planning tools or arrangements.

- Avoid salespeople who give the impression that AARP is selling or endorsing their products. AARP does not endorse any living trust product.

- Do your homework. Get information about your local probate laws from the Clerk (or Register) of Wills.

- If you opt for a living trust, make sure it's properly funded — that is, that the property has been transferred from your name to the trust. If the transfers aren't done properly, the trust will be invalid and the state will determine who inherits your property and serves as guardian for your minor children.

- If someone tries to sell you a living trust, ask if the seller is an attorney. Some states limit the sale of living trust services to attorneys.

- Remember the Cooling Off Rule. If you buy a living trust in your home or somewhere other than the seller's permanent place of business (say, at a hotel seminar), the seller must give you a written statement of your right to cancel the deal within three business days.

The Cooling Off Rule provides that during the sales transaction, the salesperson must give you two copies of a cancellation form (one for you to keep and one to return to the company) and a copy of your contract or receipt. The contract or receipt must be dated, show the name and address of the seller, and explain your right to cancel. You can write a letter and exercise your right to cancel within three days, even if you don't receive a cancellation form. You do not have to give a reason for canceling. Stopping payment on your check if you do cancel in these circumstances is a good idea. If you pay by credit card and the seller does not credit your account after you cancel, you can dispute the charge with the credit card issuer.

- Check out the organization with the Better Business Bureau in your state or the state where the organization is located before you send any money for any product or service. Although this is prudent, it is not foolproof: there may be no record of complaints if an organization is too new or has changed its name.

Establishing a Trust Fund

People often associate trust funds only with the wealthy. But a trust fund ("trust") actually can be an effective financial tool for many people in many circumstances.

A trust is a separate legal entity that holds property or assets of some kind for the benefit of a specific person, group of people or organization known as the beneficiary (beneficiaries). The person creating a trust is called the grantor, donor or settlor. When a trust is established, an individual or corporate entity is designated to oversee or manage the assets in the trust. This individual or entity is called a trustee. A trustee can be a professional with financial knowledge, a relative or loyal friend or a corporation. There are pluses and minuses to each type of trustee. An individual trustee may provide a more personal touch, but may die or move away. A corporate trustee may be less personal but provides experience, investment skills, permanence and impartiality. More than one trustee can be named by the grantor if he or she wishes.

Benefits of Establishing a Trust

Whether it makes sense to establish a trust depends on your individual circumstances. Some common reasons for setting up a trust include:

- To provide for minor children or family members who lack financial experience or who are unable to manage their assets

- To provide for management of your assets should you become unable to oversee them yourself

- To avoid probate and transfer your assets immediately to your beneficiaries upon death

- To reduce estate taxes or provide liquid assets to help pay for them.

Keep in mind that you may not need to establish a trust to accomplish these and other financial goals. A well-written will may distribute your assets appropriately. Check with a lawyer before deciding if a trust is right for you.

Types of Trusts

There are two basic forms of trusts: after-death (or testamentary) and living (or inter vivos).

An after-death trust will come into existence, usually by virtue of a will, after a person's death. The assets to fund these trusts must usually go through the probate process. In certain states they may be court- supervised even after the estate is closed. An example of an after-death trust would be a mother leaving land to a trust benefiting a young son in her will. The will establishes the trust to which the land is transferred, to be administered by a trustee until the boy reaches a stated age, at which point the land is transferred to the son outright.

A living trust, on the other hand, is a trust made while the person establishing the trust is still alive. In this case, a mother could establish a trust for her son during her lifetime, designating herself as trustee and her son as beneficiary. As the beneficiary, her son does not own the property but can receive income derived from it.

Living trusts can be revocable or irrevocable. The most popular type of trust is the revocable living trust, which allows the individual to make changes to the trust during his or her life. Revocable living trusts avoid the often lengthy probate process but, by themselves, don't provide shelter for assets from federal or state estate taxes.

When an irrevocable living trust is set up, ownership of the assets is turned over to the trustee. The trust becomes, for tax purposes, a separate entity, and the assets cannot be removed, nor can changes be made by the grantor. This type of trust often is used by individuals with large estates to reduce estate taxes and avoid probate. However, if the grantor names himself or herself as trustee or is entitled to trust income, the tax benefits would generally be lost.

Specific-Use Trusts

Before you set up a trust, ask yourself what you are trying to accomplish. Here are just a few of the many special uses for trusts:

- A *charitable trust* is used to make donations and realize tax savings for an estate. Typically, there is a transfer of property such as art or real estate to a trust which continues to hold the asset until it is transferred to the charity, usually after your death. The donor can continue to enjoy the use of the property, then the charitable gift may be deductible for estate tax purposes.

"The most popular type of trust is the revocable living trust, which allows the individual to make changes to the trust during his or her life."

- A *bypass trust* allows a married couple, in certain cases, to shelter more of their estate from estate taxes. The first spouse to die can leave assets in a trust which can provide income to the surviving spouse for the rest of his or her life, taking advantage of the unified credit provided under Federal Gift and Estate Tax law. Upon the death of the second spouse, the assets in the trust pass directly to the children or other beneficiaries, without being taxed at the second spouse's death.

- A *spendthrift* trust can be a good idea if your beneficiary is too young or does not have the mental capacity to handle money. The trust can be established so that the beneficiary receives small amounts of money at specified intervals. It is designed to prevent that person from squandering money or losing the principal in a bad investment.

- A *life insurance trust* is often used to give your estate liquidity. In this case, the proceeds are payable to the trust and the trustee is empowered to lend money to or purchase assets from the estate.

Establishing a Trust

Establishing a trust requires a document that specifies your wishes, lists beneficiaries, names a trustee or trustees to manage the assets and describes what the trustee or trustees may do. For a living trust, you can name yourself as trustee but, if you do, you should also name a successor trustee to take over if you should become disabled or when you die. Once the document is completed, you must transfer the assets to the trust. Keep in mind that, in the case of certain assets, such as real estate, you may incur fees and transfer taxes.

Some states require you to file a trust document with the state. To find out about your state's laws regarding trusts, talk with an attorney who specializes in estate planning.

The Role of the Trustee

The person who manages a trust, the trustee, has a legal duty to manage the trust's assets in the best interests of the beneficiary or beneficiaries. This might include managing rental properties, investing funds or paying income to the beneficiary.

How much a trustee is required to do and how much access he or she has to the funds should be specified in the trust. A simple or mandatory trust requires the trustee to distribute income to the beneficiary. A complex or discretionary trust may afford the trustee discretion over the principal and income to be distributed.

Generally, trustees are paid for their services because of the amount of work involved in managing a trust and the threat of potential liability if assets are mismanaged. Institutions such as banks or trust companies usually charge a percentage of the trust's value to handle the management (accounting, investing, distributions, etc.) of the trust. The percentage will vary depending upon the size and complexity of the trust. Individual trustees often receive a flat fee or hourly rate. No matter how a trustee is to be paid, it should be agreed upon in advance.

If you want to name someone as a trustee, talk with that individual or entity about the trust. Be sure they agree to serve as trustee and can comply with the terms of the trust. Because there is generally such a high standard of duty and liability imposed on trustees, an individual or entity cannot be forced into becoming a trustee just because he or she is named in a trust document or will. If your designated trustee is unable or unwilling to perform, the court will appoint a trustee for you, unless a successor trustee, such as a corporate trustee, is designated.

Providing Peace of Mind

It's possible that a trust may be the answer to your estate planning needs. Take the time to evaluate carefully what you are trying to accomplish, then consult an attorney experienced in estate planning. A well-written trust can help to provide peace of mind for you and your beneficiaries.

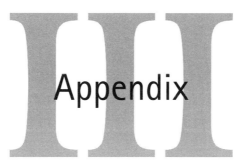

Appendix

Famous
Quotes

Thoughts on money and investing by some well-known individuals.

"The easiest way for your children to learn about money is for you not to have any."

~ Katharine Whitehorn

"It is pretty hard to tell what does bring happiness; poverty and wealth have both failed."

~ Kin Hubbard (1868 - 1930)

"The safest way to double your money is to fold it over and put it in your pocket."

~ Kin Hubbard (1868 - 1930)

"There's no secret about success. Did you ever know a successful man who didn't tell you about it?"

~ Kin Hubbard (1868 - 1930)

"Too many of us look upon Americans as dollar chasers. This is a cruel libel, even if it is reiterated thoughtlessly by the Americans themselves."

~ Albert Einstein (1879 - 1955)

"He that is of the opinion money will do everything may well be suspected of doing everything for money."

~ Benjamin Franklin (1706 - 1790)

"If you would be wealthy, think of saving as well as getting."

~ Benjamin Franklin (1706 - 1790)

"Time is money."

~ Benjamin Franklin

"Annual income twenty pounds, annual expenditure nineteen six, result happiness. Annual income twenty pounds, annual expenditure twenty pound ought and six, result misery."

~ Charles Dickens (1812 - 1870)
~ David Copperfield, 1849

"If all the rich people in the world divided up their money among themselves there wouldn't be enough to go around."

~ Christina Stead (1903 - 1983)
House of All Nations (1938) "Credo"

"Endless money forms the sinews of war."

~ Cicero (106 BC - 43 BC), Philippics

"Money was never a big motivation for me, except as a way to keep score. The real excitement is playing the game."

~ Donald Trump (1946 -),
"Trump: Art of the Deal"

"If you want to know what God thinks of money, just look at the people he gave it to."

~ Dorothy Parker (1893 - 1967)

"Money is the sinew of love as well as war."

~ Dr. Thomas Fuller (1654 - 1734),
Gnomologia, 1732

"I'm living so far beyond my income that we may almost be said to be living apart."

~ E E Cummings (1894 - 1962)

"Save a little money each month and at the end of the year you'll be surprised at how little you have."

~ Ernest Haskins

"My problem lies in reconciling my gross habits with my net income."

~ Errol Flynn (1909 - 1959)

"Lack of money is the root of all evil."

~ George Bernard Shaw (1856 - 1950)

"One must be poor to know the luxury of giving."

~ George Eliot (1819 - 1880)

"Money frees you from doing things you dislike. Since I dislike doing nearly everything, money is handy."

~ Groucho Marx (1890 - 1977)

"The chief value of money lies in the fact that one lives in a world in which it is overestimated."

~ H. L. Mencken (1880 - 1956)

"Make money your god and it will plague you like the devil."

~ Henry Fielding (1707 - 1754)

"If you can count your money, you don't have a billion dollars."

~ J. Paul Getty (1892 - 1976)

"I have enough money to last me the rest of my life, unless I buy something."

~ Jackie Mason (1934 -)

"A large income is the best recipe for happiness I ever heard of."

~ Jane Austen (1775 - 1817)

"Nothing amuses me more than the easy manner with which everybody settles the abundance of those who have a great deal less than themselves."

~ Jane Austen (1775 - 1817), Mansfield Park

"A wise man should have money in his head, but not in his heart."

~ Jonathan Swift (1667 - 1745)

"Do not be fooled into believing that because a man is rich he is necessarily smart. There is ample proof to the contrary."

~ Julius Rosenwald (1862 - 1932)

"Be rich to yourself and poor to your friends."

~ Juvenal (55 AD - 127 AD)

"It is not easy for men to rise whose qualities are thwarted by poverty."

~ Juvenal (55 AD - 127 AD), Satires

"I don't know the key to success, but the key to failure is trying to please everybody."

~ Bill Cosby (1937 -)

"What's money? A man is a success if he gets up in the morning and goes to bed at night and in between does what he wants to do."

~ Bob Dylan (1941 -)

"The person who makes a success of living is the one who see his goal steadily and aims for it unswervingly. That is dedication."

~ Cecil B. DeMille (1881 - 1959)

"There is only one success - to be able to spend your life in your own way."

~ Christopher Morley (1890 - 1957)

"The man of virtue makes the difficulty to be overcome his first business, and success only a subsequent consideration."

~ Confucius (551 BC - 479 BC),
The Confucian Analects

"Real success is finding your lifework in the work that you love."

~ David McCullough (1933 -)

"Success in business requires training and discipline and hard work. But if you're not frightened by these things, the opportunities are just as great today as they ever were."

~ David Rockefeller (1915 -)

"Aim for success, not perfection. Never give up your right to be wrong, because then you will lose the ability to learn new things and move forward with your life."

~ Dr. David M. Burns

"Each success only buys an admission ticket to a more difficult problem."

~ Henry Kissinger (1923 -),
Wilson Library Bulletin, (1979)

"I can't give you a sure-fire formula for success, but I can give you a formula for failure: try to please everybody all the time."

~ Herbert Bayard Swope (1882 - 1958)

"The toughest thing about success is that you've got to keep on being a success. Talent is only a starting point in this business. You've got to keep on working that talent. Someday I'll reach for it and it won't be there."

~ Irving Berlin (1888 - 1989), 1958

"If you wish success in life, make perseverance your bosom friend, experience your wise counselor, caution your elder brother and hope your guardian genius."

~ Joseph Addison (1672 - 1719)

"A successful individual typically sets his next goal somewhat but not too much above his last achievement. In this way he steadily raises his level of aspiration."

~ Kurt Lewin (1890 - 1947)

"All you need in this life is ignorance and confidence; then success is sure."

~ Mark Twain (1835 - 1910),
Letter to Mrs Foote, (1887)

"People fail forward to success."

~ Mary Kay Ash

"Riches cover a multitude of woes."

~ Menander (342 BC - 292 BC),
Lady of Andros

"Whenever I hear, 'It can't be done,' I know I'm close to success."

~ Michael Flatley (Lord of the Dance)
quoted by Eric Celeste

"No matter how rich you become, how famous or powerful, when you die the size of your funeral will still pretty much depend on the weather."

~ Michael Pritchard

"It is better to have a permanent income than to be fascinating."

~ Oscar Wilde (1854 - 1900),
The Model Millionaire, 1912

"Wealth is the parent of luxury and indolence, and poverty of meanness and viciousness, and both of discontent."

~ Plato (427 BC - 347 BC), The Republic

"Money is the opposite of the weather. Nobody talks about it, but everybody does something about it."

~ Rebecca Johnson, in 'Vogue'

"Finance is the art of passing money from hand to hand until it finally disappears."

~ Robert W. Sarnoff

"It has been said that the love of money is the root of all evil. The want of money is so quite as truly."

~ Samuel Butler (1835 - 1902),
Erewhon (1872)

"A billion here, a billion there, pretty soon it adds up to real money."

~ Senator Everett Dirksen (1896 - 1969)

"The art of living easily as to money is to pitch your scale of living one degree below your means."

~ Sir Henry Taylor

"A little wonton money, which burned out the bottom of his purse."

~ Sir Thomas More (1478 - 1535),
Works

"Money: There's nothing in the world so demoralizing as money."

~ Sophocles (496 BC - 406 BC),
Antigone

"Money can't buy friends, but it can get you a better class of enemy."

~ Spike Milligan

"Man is so made that he can only find relaxation from one kind of labor by taking up another."

~ Anatole France (1844 - 1924),
The Crime of Sylvestre Bonnard

"Opportunities are usually disguised as hard work, so most people don't recognize them."

~ Ann Landers (1918 - 2002)

"Pleasures in the job put perfection in the work."

~ Aristotle (384 BC - 322 BC)

"Real success is finding your lifework in the work that you love."

~ David McCullough (1933 -)

"When a man tells you that he got rich through hard work, ask him: 'Whose?'"

~ Don Marquis (1878 - 1937)

"A human being must have occupation if he or she is not to become a nuisance to the world."

~ Dorothy L. Sayers (1893 - 1957)

"Hard work never killed anybody, but why take a chance?"

~ Edgar Bergen (1903 - 1978)
(Charlie McCarthy)

"People forget how fast you did a job – but they remember how well you did it."

~ Howard Newton

"Money talks...but all mine ever says is good-bye."

~ Anon.

"In its famous paradox, the equation of money and excrement, psychoanalysis becomes the first science to state what common sense and the poets have long known – that the essence of money is in its absolute worthlessness."

~ Norman O. Brown

"The entire essence of America is the hope to first make money -- then make money with money..."

~ Paul Erdman

"Money is like manure. You have to spread it around or it smells."

~ J. Paul Getty

"Money, the root of all evil...but the cure for all sadness."

~ Mike Gill

"So you think that money is the root of all evil. Have you ever asked what is the root of all money?"

~ Ayn Rand

"Money is the barometer of a society's virtue."

~ Ayn Rand

"Sudden money is going from zero to two hundred dollars a week. The rest doesn't count."

~ Neil Simon

"Money is the most egalitarian force in society. It confers power on whoever holds it."

~ Roger Starr

"Money may kindle, but it cannot by itself, and for very long, burn."

~ Igor Stravinski

Success

"We succeed only as we identify in life, or in war, or in anything else, a single overriding objective, and make all other considerations bend to that one objective."

~ Dwight D. Eisenhower (1890 - 1969),
speech (1957)

"Success is counted sweetest by those who ne'er succeed."

~ Emily Dickinson (1830 - 1886)

"Success didn't spoil me, I've always been insufferable."

~ Fran Lebowitz (1950 -)

"Nothing changes your opinion of a friend so surely as success - yours or his."

~ Franklin P. Jones,
Saturday Evening Post, (1953)

"I owe my success to having listened respectfully to the very best advice, and then going away and doing the exact opposite."

~ G. K. Chesterton (1874 - 1936)

"Nothing fails like success."

~ Gerald Nachman

"To freely bloom - that is my definition of success."

~ Gerry Spence,
How to Argue and Win Every Time

"My mother drew a distinction between achievement and success. She said that 'achievement is the knowledge that you have studied and worked hard and done the best that is in you. Success is being praised by others, and that's nice, too, but not as important or satisfying. Always aim for achievement and forget about success."

~ Helen Hayes (1900 - 1993)

"Men are born to succeed, not fail."

~ Henry David Thoreau (1817 - 1862)

"Success usually comes to those who are too busy to be looking for it."

~ Henry David Thoreau (1817 - 1862)

Wealth

"The real measure of your wealth is how much you'd be worth if you lost all your money."

~ Anon.

"If you can count your money, you don't have a billion dollars."

~ J. Paul Getty

"I'd like to live as a poor man with lots of money."

~ Pablo Picasso

"A fool and his money are soon parted."

~ Thomas Tusser,
Five Hundred Points of Good Husbandry

"Don't try to buy at the bottom and sell at the top. It can't be done except by liars."

~ Bernard Baruch

"A market is the combined behavior of thousands of people responding to information, misinformation and whim."

~ Kenneth Chang

"Emotions are your worst enemy in the stock market."

~ Don Hays

"Everyone has the brainpower to follow the stock market. If you made it through fifth-grade math, you can do it."

~ Peter Lynch,
Modern Maturity Magazine, (1995)

"90% of the people in the stock market, professionals and amateurs alike, simply haven't done enough homework."

~ William J. O'Neil

"I have probably purchased fifty 'hot tips' in my career, maybe even more. When I put them all together, I know I am a net loser."

~ Charles Schwab

"The problem with the person who thinks he's a long-term investor and impervious to short-term gyrations is that the emotion of fear and pain will eventually make him sell badly."

~ Robert Wibbelsman

Freedom

"If you make a living, if you earn your own money, you're free -- however free one can be on this planet."

~ Theodore White

Golf

"Golf is the cruelest game, because eventually it will drag you out in front of the whole school, take your lunch money and slap you around."

~ Rick Reilly

Investment

"Bulls make money. Bears make money. Pigs get slaughtered."

~ Anon.

"I made my money by selling too soon."

~ Bernard Baruch

Media

"The function of the press in society is to inform, but its role in society is to make money."

~ A. J. Liebling, The Press, 1961

Taxation

"The politicians don't just want your money. They want your soul. They want you to be worn down by taxes until you are dependent and helpless. When you subsidize poverty and failure, you get more of both."

~ James Dale Davidson

Promises to Keep:
An Interview of Financial and Estate Planning with Kelly Financial Services

"We work with the affluent and their families, business owners and professionals and those at or near retirement. We work diligently and tirelessly to preserve assets through estate planning, smart strategies and sound management."

– William Kelly

With this pledge to all of his clients, William Kelly labors at Kelly Financial Services in Braintree, specializing in estate planning, insurance and retirement planning.

Q Who would benefit from your services?

A We work with seniors, business owners and professional people who are at or near retirement. Our clients need help with retirement plans and estate planning. We generally work with affluent people, but that is not a qualifier. We help everyone who comes through our door.

Q What programs do you recommend to seniors?

A We have developed a program entitled Senior Safe Money Strategies℠. This program guarantees returns with no losses of principle due to risks. It is suitable for people willing to accept a 3 to 14 percent return, with a guaranteed minimum and no risk of principal. None of my clients have ever lost principal due to risk. That does not mean it will never happen, But it has not happened up until now.

Q What special concerns apply to seniors when it comes to financial planning?

A There are five T's that work against seniors financially. They are as follows:

- Time: Seniors do not have time to rebound from a sudden market downturn or financial loss.

- Technology: The markets once became overpriced due to the overvaluation of the technology sector. That led to a crash in 2001.

- Taxation: Since 1983, some of the largest tax increases in our nation have occurred for those ages 62 and over. This is due in part to their social security being taxed at an increasingly higher rate.

- Television: Sponsored financial broadcasts tend to tout securities. The message is, "BUY! BUY! BUY!" There is seldom a message to sell. For people over 60, I think avoiding a loss is more important than risking a gain.

- Terrorism: Terrorism is capable of rattling, paralyzing, or shutting down the market. It has created unprecedented volatility.

Q How does your Senior Safe Money Strategies℠ address the five T's?

A Our clients do not have to read the headlines and wonder if they're going to have a good day investment-wise. They are likely to have a little more money each day regardless of what is going on in the world.

Q What is the greatest financial concern for seniors today?

A Seniors are concerned about not being a burden to others and not having to depend upon family or welfare to survive. Secondly, they are concerned with preserving assets, having something to pass along to the next generation. This is our specialized area. I work to align assets, minimize risk and help seniors grow their assets. Our affiliated attorneys work to preserve and pass family assets and protect them from the costs of catastrophic illness and spend down. Generally, 80% of the medical expenses a person incurs in a lifetime occur in the last 3 years of their life. These expenses can wipe out an estate quickly if the planning wasn't done properly. We make sure, whenever possible, nursing home costs and other expenses due to illness do not eat up out clients' estates.

Q **What are some concerns seniors have regarding probate?**

A There are five fears seniors have concerning probate: First, it is a public event, subject to intrusions. Second, it is costly. Third, it is time-consuming. Fourth, it is subject to being contested. And fifth, the laws and limits are constantly changing. We provide expert guidance, and a competent legal team, to protect our clients during the probate process.

Q **What other financial concerns do seniors have?**

A Bloodline planning. We help many clients establish trusts to preserve and pass assets on to the next generation. Many clients want bloodline planning, so taxes, the government, or predators do not invade their assets.

Q **What is your main concern when it comes to your clients?**

A Our focus is to do the right thing, everyday for our all of our clients.

When Your Broker Calls, Take Notes!

A brief, quick reference document that captures some very important information.

Name of Broker: _____

Company: _____

Company Location: _____ Date: _____ Time: _____

  ❑ Phone call   ❑ Meeting

Meeting Location:

It was Recommended that I:

  ❑ Buy   ❑ Sell   ❑ Hold

Name of security discussed:

How does this recommendation meet my investment objectives? What are the specific reasons why I should invest in this? (Or sell this?)

_____

What are the specific risks if I buy or sell this investment?

_____

I asked to receive written information about this investment before making a decision:

  ❑ Yes   ❑ No

I asked for:

  ❑ A prospectus   ❑ Any other recent report (8K)

  ❑ Most recent annual report (10K) ❑ Any other available written material or brochure

  ❑ Most recent quarterly report (10Q) ❑ Other

After looking at the written material, I decided to:

  ❑ Buy
  How much? _____ At what price? _____

  ❑ Sell
  How much? _____ At what price? _____

  ❑ Do nothing

The total cost of this transaction will be:

_____

Protect Yourself In Six Ways With FDIC Insurance

If you or your family have less than $100,000 in all your deposit accounts at the same insured institution, you don't need to worry about your insurance coverage. But if you have funds at one institution totaling $100,000 or more, and if it's important to you that all your funds be insured, here's a sensible approach for protecting yourself.

1. Make a listing of all your bank accounts at the bank. "If you expect to conduct a thorough, accurate review of your deposit insurance," says Lesylee Sullivan, an FDIC insurance claims specialist in Dallas, "you need to aware of all the accounts your family owns at an institution, the types of accounts, and the names of the beneficiaries." She notes that the beneficiaries especially matter with payable-on-death (POD) accounts because a spouse, child, grandchild, parent or sibling qualify the account for extra insurance but other relatives don't.

2. Read the FDIC pamphlet "Your Insured Deposit." This book, the FDIC's primary consumer publication devoted to deposit insurance, explains the rules in a simple, question-and-answer format. Contact FDIC, Public Information Center for details about how to obtain a copy:

   801 17th Street, NW,
   Room 100, Washington, DC 20434
   Phone: 800-276-6003 or 202-416-6940

3. Consider asking "EDIE," the FDIC's Electronic Deposit Insurance Estimator. This interactive website estimates your coverage based on your answers to a series of questions about your accounts. EDIE is simple to use and can be accessed at the FDIC's web site, www.fdic.gov, 24 hours a day, seven days a week, at Electronic Deposit Insurance Estimator.

4. Double check with an FDIC expert. Helping depositors and bankers with deposit insurance questions is a big part of the FDIC's work. So, for peace of mind, it's smart to get an independent confirmation of the insurance rules and your insurance status from the FDIC. Call 800-276-6003 to learn more.

5. Make adjustments to your accounts, if necessary, to bring them within the insurance limit. In general, there are two options for fully insuring deposits over $100,000.

   First option: You can divide the funds among various types of accounts at the same institution, because different categories are separately insured to $100,000, but this is an option you need to think about carefully. "It means you are changing the legal ownership of the funds, either now or upon your death, just to increase your insurance coverage," says Kathleen Nagle, a supervisor with the agency's Division of Compliance and Consumer Affairs in Washington. "Before you do that, you should understand how a change in account category affects your rights and the rights of any beneficiaries to your funds." Example: You can shift some funds from a payable-on-death account to a joint account, but be aware that co-owners of your joint account will be able to access the money while you are alive.

   Second option: You can move funds in excess of $100,000 to accounts at other insured institutions, and keep no more than $100,000 at each institution. This option works well for people who don't want, or don't qualify for, another type of account at their existing bank. Moving some funds to another bank also is a good choice for people who just aren't sure how the insurance rules allow them to keep more than $100,000 at one bank and still be fully protected, adds Washington-based attorney Christopher Hencke. "Your safest approach," he says, "is to divide your funds among several insured banks so that your total funds at any one bank do not exceed $100,000."

6. Periodically review your insurance coverage. A one-time checkup on your deposit insurance coverage isn't enough for individuals or families with close to or more than $100,000 at one institution. We suggest to take another look: Before you open a new account. Follow the steps described previously to find out what effect the new account would have on your insurance coverage. FDIC Chicago attorney Christine Tullio also suggests that you keep a list of the accounts that you and other family members hold at one institution, so you can easily remember which accounts to figure into your insurance calculations. After the death of a loved one. The rules allow a six-month grace period after a depositor's death to give survivors or estate planners a chance to restructure accounts. If you fail to act within six months, you run the risk of, say, joint accounts becoming part of the survivor's individual accounts, and that could put the funds over the $100,000 limit.

If a large windfall comes your way.

If you sell your house or receive a large payment from a trust, a pension, a lawsuit or an insurance claim, make sure any deposits, especially those made on your behalf by third parties, won't put you over the $100,000 limit.

If you own accounts at two institutions that merge, and the combined funds exceed $100,000.

Accounts at the two institutions before the merger would continue to be separately insured for six months after the merger, and longer for some CDs, but you have to remember to review the accounts within the grace period to avoid a potential problem with excess funds.

If a Bank Fails:

Answers to common questions about an uncommon event.

What happens to "uninsured" deposits -- those over the $100,000 insurance limit?

First, remember that all deposits within the $100,000 insurance limit are always fully protected. Also, in most cases, the FDIC will arrange with another institution to acquire your failed bank, and you will have immediate access to your insured funds by check, automated teller machine, debit card and other services.

But if your bank fails and you have funds exceeding the $100,000 insurance limit, the FDIC will start by giving you a document called a "receivership certificate" indicating the amount of your uninsured deposits. Then, depending on various factors -- including the cost of the bank failure minus how much the FDIC recovers liquidating your bank's assets -- you still can recover some or, in rare circumstances, all of your uninsured funds. The liquidation process can take several years, so it's important for uninsured depositors to make sure the FDIC has your correct address.

What if I have a cashier's check (or any other official check) from a failed bank?

Until a cashier's check, money order, interest check or other official check is cashed or deposited elsewhere and it "clears" the bank it is drawn on, the funds are still considered to be on deposit at that bank. So, if that bank fails before the check clears, the FDIC will combine the amount of the check with your other deposit accounts in the same ownership category, and the combined total will be insured to $100,000.

Example: You have a $125,000 savings account at XYZ Bank and you withdraw $75,000 in the form of a cashier's check. But before you deposit the check at another bank and the check clears, XYZ Bank fails. Your $75,000 cashier's check from XYZ Bank gets combined with the amount in your account there for insurance purposes, resulting in a $125,000 balance again and $25,000 uninsured.

What happens to my direct deposits?

If a failed bank is acquired by another bank, all direct deposits, including Social Security checks or paychecks delivered electronically, will be automatically deposited into your account at the assuming bank.

If the FDIC cannot find an acquirer for the failed bank, the FDIC will arrange with another local bank to temporarily process any direct deposits until you can make new arrangements for direct deposits as well as automatic withdrawals (such as automatic payments to utilities or insurance companies) with other banks.

How can I access my safe deposit box?

If the FDIC finds a new owner for a bank where you have a safe deposit box, you will be able to conduct business as usual. If the FDIC cannot find a buyer for your bank, we will mail instructions to you that will explain how you can remove the contents of your box.

What happens to any loans I have at the failed bank?

If your bank fails and you have funds exceeding the $100,000 insurance limit, you can still recover some or, in rare circumstances, all of your uninsured funds.

You remain liable for any payments due on a loan or credit card. You would continue making payments as you did before the bank failed until you are instructed to do otherwise in writing by the acquiring bank or the FDIC.

If your loan is delinquent and you have insured deposits at the bank, the FDIC may "set off" (deduct) the loan balance from your insurance payment. However, the FDIC will only deduct past-due money if the loan and the deposit account involve the same people. As an example, if you are delinquent on a loan that is in your name only, the FDIC may not deduct funds from a deposit account you own jointly with another person.

How can I get more information about what happens when a bank fails?

Start at the FDIC's Web site. Among the special services available online: updated information about individual bank failures dating back to October 2000 and a searchable database of unclaimed funds from failed financial institutions.

Investment Swindles: How They Work and How to Avoid Them.

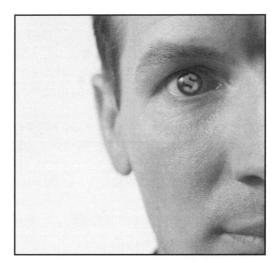

Americans are investors. We purchase stocks and bonds, contribute to savings programs, own real estate, participate in futures and options markets, acquire collectibles, provide start-up capital for new business ventures, buy franchises, and the list goes on. The strength of our economy is in large measure the product of our combined investments.

Perhaps more so than any people in the world, we enjoy an ever-expanding variety of investments to choose from, coupled with the freedom to make our own investment decisions. It's our money and we can invest it as we wish.

Unfortunately, some unscrupulous promoters abuse our freedom to choose by concocting investment schemes that have zero possibility of making money for anyone other than themselves. Such persons promise investment rewards they cannot possibly deliver and have no intention of delivering.

They are swindlers.

Many of them are very good at it. Their annual take through lying and deceit is in the billions of dollars. If one estimate of $10 billion a year lost to investment fraud is accurate, that's more money than the combined annual profits of the nation's three major automakers! Some say even that estimate may be too low.

Successful investment swindlers use every trick in the book, and some that aren't even recorded, to convince you that none of the descriptions and precautions in the following pages apply to them. After all, they are offering you a once-in-a-lifetime opportunity to make a lot of money quickly and you do trust them, don't you? As will be seen, some of their methods of gaining your trust are truly ingenious.

Who are the Investment Swindlers?

They are a faceless voice on a telephone. Or a friend of a friend. They may perform surgery on their victims' savings from a dingy back office or boiler-room or from an opulent suite in the new bank building. They may wear three-piece suits or they may wear hard hats. They may have no apparent connection to the investment business or they may have an alphabet-soup of impressive letters following their names. They may be glib and fast-talking or so seemingly shy and soft-spoken that you feel almost compelled to force your money on them.

The first rule of protecting yourself from an investment swindle is thus to rid yourself of any notions you might have as to what an investment swindler looks like or sounds like. Indeed, some swindlers don't start out to be swindlers. There are case histories in which individuals who held positions of trust and esteem-accountants, attorneys, bona fide investment brokers and even

"He that is of the opinion money will do everything may well be suspected of doing everything for money."

Benjamin Franklin

1706 – 1790

doctors-have sacrificed their ethics for the fast buck of running an investment scam.

In still other cases, investment programs that began with legitimate intentions went sour through happenstance or poor management--leading the promoter to mishandle or abscond with investors' capital. Whether an investment is planned as a scam or simply becomes one, the result is the same.

This is why, as we will discuss, protecting your savings against fraud involves at least three steps: Carefully check out the person and firm you would be dealing with; take a close and cautious look at the investment offer itself; and continue to monitor any investment that you decide to make. No one of these precautions alone may be sufficient.

Who are the Victims of Investment Fraud?

If you are absolutely certain it could never be you, the investment swindler starts with a big advantage. Investment fraud generally happens to people who think it couldn't happen to them.

Just as there is no typical profile for swindlers, neither is there one for their victims. While some scams target persons who are known or thought to have deep pockets, most swindlers take the attitude that everyone's money spends the same. It simply takes more small investors to fund a large fraud. In fact, some swindlers deliberately seek out families that may have limited means or financial difficulties--figuring such persons may be particularly receptive to a proposal that offers fast

and large profits. A favorite pitch is that small investors can become rich only if they learn and employ the investment strategies used by wealthy persons. Naturally, the swindler will teach them!

Although victims of investment fraud can differ from one another in many ways, they do, unfortunately, have one trait in common: Greed that exceeds their caution. Plus a willingness to believe what they want to believe. Movie actors and athletes, professional persons and successful business executives, political leaders and internationally famous economists have all fallen victim to investment fraud. So have hundreds of thousands of others, including widows, retirees and working people--people who made their money the hard way and lost it the fast way.

How Investment Swindlers Find (or Attract) Their Victims

Swindlers attempt to mimic the sales approaches of legitimate investment firms and salespersons. Thus, the fact that someone may contact you in a particular way--by phone, mail, or even through a referral--should not in itself be viewed as an indication that the investment is or isn't shady. Many totally reputable firms also use the same methods to effectively and economically identify individuals who may have an interest in their investment products and services.

Bearing in mind that investigate before you invest is good advice no matter how you are approached, these are some of the methods con men commonly employ to contact their victims-to-be.

• Telephone

So-called telephone boiler-rooms remain a favorite way for swindlers and their sales squads to quickly contact large numbers of potential investors. Even if a swindler has to make 100 or 200 phone calls to find a mooch (one of the terms swindlers use for their victims), he figures that the opportunity to pocket thousands of dollars of someone's savings is still good pay for the time and cost involved.

• Mail

Some sellers of fraudulent investment deals buy bona fide mailing lists--names and addresses of persons who, for example, subscribe to a particular investment-related publication, who have responded to previous direct mail offers, or who have other characteristics that swindlers look for. In the hope of avoiding notice by postal authorities, mail order swindlers may not make a direct or immediate pitch for your money. Rather, they often seek to entice you to write or phone for more information. Then comes a call from the salesperson or the person who closes the deal. Some may phone even if you didn't respond to the mailing.

• Advertisements

A newspaper or magazine ad may offer (or at least hint at) profit opportunities far more attractive than available through conventional investments. Once you've taken the bait, the swindler will then attempt to "set the hook." Even though investment crooks know that regulatory agencies regularly monitor ads in major publications, some nevertheless use such publications in the hope of being able to hit-and-run before an investigator shows up. Others advertise in narrowly circulated publications they think regulators may be less likely to see.

• Referrals

One of the oldest schemes going involves paying fast, large profits to initial investors (actually from their own or other peoples' investments) knowing that they are likely to recommend the investment to their friends. And these friends will tell their friends. Soon, the swindler no longer needs to find new victims; they will find him.

• The "Reputable" Business

Some swindlers go first class. Using profits from previous swindles, they rent plush offices, hire an interior decorator and professional-sounding receptionist and open what has the appearance--but not the reality of a reputable investment firm. You may even have to phone for an appointment, and once there don't be surprised to be kept waiting (that's intended to make you all the more eager). This kind of swindler's success depends on how long he can keep his victims from knowing they are being cheated. Investors are assured that their large profits are being reinvested to earn even larger profits. Such a swindler may join local civic groups, contribute to charities, and generally play the role of solid citizen.

Techniques Investment Swindlers Use

Their techniques are as varied as their methods of establishing contact. If there is a common denominator, however, it is their ability to be convincing. The skills that make them successful are essentially the same skills that enable any good salesperson to be successful.

But swindlers have a decided advantage: They don't have to make good on their promises. In the absence of this responsibility, they have no reluctance to promise whatever it takes to persuade you to part with your money. These are some of their techniques:

• *Expectation of Large Profits*

The profits a swindler talks about are generally large enough to make you interested and eager to invest--but not so large as to make you overly skeptical. Or he may mention a profit figure he thinks you will consider believable and then, as a further enticement, suggest that the potential profit is actually far greater than that. The latter figure, of course, is the one he hopes you will focus on. Generally speaking, if an investment proposal sounds too good to be true, it probably is.

• *Low Risk*

Some are so blatant as to suggest there's no risk--that the investment is a sure money maker. Obviously, the last thing a swindler wants you to think about is the possibility of losing your money. (If you ask how you can be certain your money is safe, you can count on a plausible-sounding answer. Besides, at this point, he figures you will believe what you want to believe.)

To make his pitch more credible, a swindler may acknowledge that there

could be some risk--then quickly assure you it's minimal in relation to the profits you will almost certainly make. A con man may become impatient or even aggressive if the question of risk is raised--perhaps suggesting that he has better things to do than waste time with people who lack the courage and foresight needed to make money! With this kind of put down, he hopes you won't bring up the subject again.

• *Urgency*

There's usually some compelling reason why it's essential for you to invest right now. Perhaps because the investment opportunity can "be offered to only a limited number of people." Or because delaying the investment could mean missing out on a large profit (after all, once the information he has confided to you becomes generally known, the price is sure to go up, right?).

Urgency is important to a swindler. For one thing, he wants your money as quickly as possible with a minimum of effort on his part. And he doesn't want you to have time to think it over, discuss it with someone who might suggest you become suspicious, or check him or his proposal out with a regulatory agency. Besides, he may not plan on remaining in town very long.

• *Confidence*

They don't call them con men for nothing! They sound confident about the money you are going to make so that you will become confident enough to let go of your savings. Their message is that they are doing you a favor by offering the investment opportunity. A swindler may even threaten (pleasantly or otherwise) to end the discussion by suggesting that if you are not really interested there are many other people who will be. Once you protest that you are interested, he figures your savings are practically in his pocket.

Although you can't necessarily spot a con man by the way he talks, most are strong-willed, articulate individuals who will dominate the conversation-even if they do it in a low-key, friendly sort of way. The more they talk, the less chance you have to ask questions.

Several Investment Swindles and How They Worked

There's a saying among swindlers that it's not the scam that counts, it's the sell. Judging from the number of arcane and often outlandish schemes that have been employed to separate otherwise prudent people from their money, the saying would seem to reflect reality. The evidence is that if people can be made believers, they can be sold practically anything. Consider several of the ways in which hustlers of phony investments have won the confidence of persons whom they planned to victimize.

The Old-Fashioned Ponzi Scheme

It's become one of the oldest and most often employed investment schemes because it's proven to be one of the most lucrative. While there are innumerable variations, here is how a person we will call Frank C. practiced it. At the outset, Frank approached a relatively small number of influential persons in the community and offered them the opportunity to invest--with a guaranteed high return--in a computer-generated program of arbitrage in foreign currency fluctuations. To be sure, it sounded high tech and sophisticated but Frank had his eye on sophisticated and well-heeled victims.

Within a short period of time, he approached and sold the scheme to still other investors-then promptly used a portion of the money invested by these persons to pay large profits to the original group of investors. As word spread of Frank's genius for making money and paying profits, even more would-be investors anxiously put up even larger sums of money. Some of it was used to recycle the fictitious profit payments and, like a pebble in the water, the word of fast and fabulous rewards produced an ever-widening circle of eager investors. And more money poured in.

And Frank C. left town a wealthy man.

The Infallible Forecaster

Jim L. (among his many aliases) had a full-time job in the daytime, but with assets that consisted only of a phone, patience and an easy way of talking he managed to parlay a nighttime sideline into an ill-gotten fortune. The routine went like this.

Jim would phone someone we'll call Mrs. Smith and quickly assure her that, "No," he didn't want her to invest a single cent. "Never invest with someone you don't know," he preached. But he said he would like to demonstrate his firm's "research skill" by sharing with her the forecast that so-and-so a commodity was about to experience a significant price increase. Sure enough, the price soon went up.

A second phone call didn't solicit an investment either. Jim simply wanted to share with Mrs. Smith a prediction that the price of so-and-so a commodity was about to go down. "Our forecasts will help you decide whether ours is the kind of firm you might someday want to invest with," he added. As predicted, the price of the commodity subsequently declined.

By the time Mrs. Smith received a third call, she was a believer. She not only wanted to invest but insisted on it-- with a big enough investment to make up for the opportunities she had already missed out on.

What Mrs. Smith had no way of knowing was that Jim had begun with a calling list of 200 persons. In the first call, he told 100 that the price of so-and-so a commodity would go up and the other 100 were told it would go down. When it went up, he made a second call to the 100 who had been given the "correct forecast." Of these, 50 were told the next price move would be up and 50 were told it would be down.

The end result: Once the predicted price decline occurred, Jim had a list of 50 persons eager to invest. After all, how could they go wrong with someone so obviously infallible in forecasting prices?

But go wrong they did, the moment they decided to send Jim a half million dollars from their collective savings accounts.

All That Glitters

Not only did the two brothers have a fancy office building with their own company name on it, but the investment offer seemed sound and straightforward: "Instead of buying gold outright and holding it for appreciation, make a small downpayment that the firm could use to secure financing that would permit much larger quantities of gold to be bought and held for the investor's account." That way, when the price of gold rose--as was "sure to happen"-- investors stood to realize highly leveraged profits.

The company provided storage vaults where investors could view the wall-to-wall stacks of glittering bullion. By the time authorities caught wind of the scheme's suspicious smell and looked for themselves, it turned out the only thing gold was the color of the paint on the cardboard used to construct look-alike bars of bullion.

The counterfeit gold, however, proved far easier to find than the millions of dollars of investors' money. Most of that is still missing.

16 Questions That Can Turn Off an Investment Swindler

The first line of defense against investment fraud is your inalienable right to ask questions and--until you get the right answers--to say "No." And mean no. Not surprisingly, this is usually an investment swindler's first point of attack. To keep you from asking questions, he asks them! Invariably, the questions have "yes" answers, such as "You would at least be interested in hearing about such a fantastic investment opportunity, wouldn't you?" or "You would like to make a large amount of money in a short period of time with little or no risk, right?"

One difference between a reputable investment firm and a swindler is that reputable firms encourage you to ask questions, to obtain as much information as possible, to clearly understand the risks involved, and to be entirely comfortable with any investment decision you make. The only thing a swindler wants is your money. These are some of the questions that swindlers don't like to hear...

1.

Where did you get my name?

If the response is that you were chosen from a "select list of intelligent and prudent investors," that select list may be the telephone directory, or a purchased list of persons who've bought certain types of books, subscribed to particular magazines, or responded to newspaper ads. If you have made ill-advised investments in the past, you can be pretty sure your name is on someone's alumni list. It's the list swindlers prize most: Easy preys who are eager to recoup (but are doomed to repeat) their earlier losses.

2.

What risks are involved in the proposed investment?

Except for obligations of the U.S. Treasury, which are considered risk-free, all investments involve some degree of risk. And some investments, by their nature, involve greater risks than others. Keep in mind that if the salesman had knowledge of a sure-thing, big-profit investment opportunity, he wouldn't be on the phone talking with you.

3.

Can you send me a written explanation of your investment so I can consider it at my leisure?

For someone peddling fraudulent investments, that can be a double turnoff. For one thing, most crooks are reluctant to put anything in writing that might cause them to run afoul of postal authorities or provide material that, at some point, might become evidence in a fraud trial. Secondly, swindlers don't want you to do anything at your leisure. They want your money now.

Accordingly, it's a good rule of thumb that any investment which "absolutely has to be made immediately" shouldn't be made at all. You may not always be right, but you are less likely to be sorry.

4.

Would you mind explaining your investment proposal to some third party, such as my attorney, accountant, investment advisor or banker?

If the answer goes something along the lines of "normally, I'd be glad to, but there isn't time for that," or if the salesman snaps back by asking "can't you make your own investment decisions." these are virtually certain clues that your final answer should be an emphatic "No."

5.

Can you give me the names of your firm's principals and officers?

Although some persons who establish and operate dishonest firms change their own names as often as they change their firms' names, even the hint that you are the kind of investor who checks into things like that can be a fast turn-off for a swindler.

6.

Can you provide references?

Not just another list of other investors who supposedly became fabulously wealthy (the names you get may be the salesman's boss or someone sitting at the next phone), but reputable and reliable recommendations such as a bank or well-known brokerage firm that you can easily contact.

7.

Do you have any documents such as a prospectus or risk disclosure statement that you can provide?

This may not be available in connection with all types of investments but in many investment areas--such as securities, futures and options trading--it's required. And there can be requirements that you be provided with this information and acknowledge in writing that you have read and understood it. Obviously, it's not the sort of information a swindler is likely to distribute.

8.

Are the investments you are offering traded on a regulated exchange, such as a securities or futures exchange?

Some bona fide investments are and some aren't, but fraudulent investments never are. Exchanges have strict rules designed to assure fair dealing and competitive price determination. There are also in-place mechanisms to provide for rule enforcement and to impose severe sanctions against those who fail to observe the rules.

9.

What governmental or industry regulatory supervision is your firm subject to?

If the salesman rattles off a list that ranges from the FBI to the Boy Scouts, tell him you'd like to check the firm's good standing before making an important investment decision. Then verify the response. Few things discourage a swindler faster than the thought that his first visitor the next morning may be from a regulatory agency. If, on the other hand, you are told his particular area of investment isn't subject to regulation (perhaps because everyone in his business is an ethical, upstanding citizen), take that explanation for whatever you think it's worth. At the very least, keep in mind that any ongoing supervision which isn't being provided by a regulatory organization or agency will have to be provided by you.

10.

How long has your company been in business?

In any kind of business activity, there can be advantages to dealing with a known, established company. This isn't to say that new businesses aren't starting up all the time or that the vast majority aren't perfectly reputable. But if you find yourself talking with someone who doesn't seem to have a past, it can be worthwhile to find out why. Many swindlers have been running scams for years but understandably aren't anxious to talk about it.

11.

What has your track record been?

Before you accept a salesman's assurance that he can make money for you, you have the right to know what his performance has been in making money for others. And ask to have the information (if there is any) in writing. Boasting over the phone is one thing; putting it down on paper is quite another. In any case, even if you are able to obtain a documented performance record, don't lose sight of the fact that past performance in itself provides no assurance of future performance.

12.
When and where can I meet with you or with another representative of your firm?

Chances are a crooked operator--particularly if he is operating out of a telephone boiler-room--isn't going to take the time to visit with you and even more certainly doesn't want you to see his place of business.

13.
Where, exactly, will my money be? And what type of regular accounting statements do you provide?

In many investment areas, such as futures trading, firms are required to maintain their customers' funds in segregated accounts at all times. Any mingling of investors' funds with those of the firm or its principals is prohibited. You might also want to find out what, if any, routine outside audits the firm's account records are subject to.

14.
How much of my money would go for commissions, management fees and the like?

And ask whether there will be other costs such as interest or storage charges, or whether the investment agreement involves any type of profit sharing arrangement in which the firms' principals participate. Insist on specific answers, not glib and evasive responses such as "that's not important" or "what's really important is how much money you are going to make." And, again, get it in writing, just as you would any other type of contract.

15.
How can I liquidate (i.e. sell the item I'd be investing in) if and when I decide I want my money?

If you find that the investment is illiquid, or there would be substantial costs if liquidated, or that you are unable to get straight and solid answers, these are all things to consider in deciding whether you want to invest.

16.
If disputes should arise, how can they be resolved?

Short of having to go to court to sue someone, does the company or regulatory organization provide a mechanism for resolving disputes equitably and inexpensively through arbitration, mediation, or a reparations procedure? Aside from seeking important information, you may be able to detect whether the salesperson is uncomfortable or impatient with this line of questioning. Swindlers generally are.

Before You Invest, Investigate

Asking some or even all of the questions just suggested isn't likely to produce straight answers from a crooked investment promoter but, as indicated, the very fact that you are asking such questions can be a turn-off. Bear in mind, however, that no matter how persistently or skillfully you pose the questions, experienced con men are at least equally skilled in evading them, in providing downright dishonest answers, and in refocusing the conversation on your "tremendous profit opportunity."

Bear in mind also that, while separating you from your money is the swindler's primary goal, the very last thing he wants you to do is check him out. That could cause you not to invest or, worse still, alert regulators that someone they know well has set up shop in a new area or is running a new scam.

For this reason, most con men deliberately make themselves difficult to investigate: By tailoring their schemes to operate in regulatory cracks where federal or national regulatory organizations may lack clear-cut jurisdiction; by operating in states or communities where authorities are known to be short-staffed or occupied with more pressing criminal activities; by changing their names or modus operandi, by stressing the urgency of the investment so you won't have time to investigate; and by targeting victims who may not know how or where to check them out.

Moreover, con men have numerous and ingenious ways of seeking to convince you there is no need to investigate. For example, your friends, neighbors or business associates invested and they made money, right? That, of course, is why ever-popular Ponzi schemes (named after the first person to perfect the referral technique) are so prevalent--and why you should never make investments based on tips, no matter how trustworthy the source.

While there is no way to know for certain whether a particular investment will make money or lose money, there is one thing you can be certain of: Any money you hand over to an investment swindler is lost the moment you part

with it. The question is, how do you check out someone who is offering what sounds like an irresistible investment offer? Here are some of the ways:

- **Find out whether the local police department or Better Business Bureau has complaints on file.**

  If so, you can make your investment decision accordingly. But be aware that the absence of local complaints doesn't necessarily mean a firm or individual is on the up-and-up. It may simply mean that investors haven't yet become aware that they've been bilked. Or it may mean you will have the distinction of becoming the first victim in town. It could also mean that other victims have been too embarrassed to report their losses. Regrettably, that's not uncommon.

- **Make a phone call to the financial editor of your local newspaper.**

  Although newspapers don't give endorsements or make investment recommendations, they may be aware of a swindler who is working a scam in the area--and may even have published a warning article that you happened to miss. Then too, if readers are being pitched with suspicious-sounding investment offers, that's something an investigative reporter might want to look into.

- **If the investment offer isn't local, don't be reluctant to make a long distance phone call or two.**

It could be that the police, Better Business Bureau or newspaper in the community where the offer is coming from will be able to provide information. Again, however, even the absence of such complaints doesn't necessarily mean the firm is legitimate. Some swindlers-- particularly telephone boiler-room operators--try to maintain a low profile in their local areas. That lessens the likelihood of their coming to the attention of local authorities; it prevents prospects from dropping by to see their operations; and it makes it more difficult for out-of-towners to discover what they are up to.

- **Check to see if your city or state has a consumer protection agency.**

  Many do. If so, there may be information there about the person or firm that's offering the investment you are interested in. In any case, the agency should be able to provide names, addresses and phone numbers of other places you can check.

- **Contact regulators.**

  The majority of individuals and companies offering investments to the public are subject to some sort of regulation--and may be subject to multiple regulation. Those which trade in futures contracts and options on futures contracts are regulated by the Commodity Futures Trading Commission, a federal agency, and by National Futures Association, an industry-wide self-

regulatory organization authorized by Congress. In the securities and securities options business, the federal regulatory agency is the Securities and Exchange Commission. There is also an industry self-regulatory organization, the National Association of Securities Dealers.

The Federal Trade Commission has jurisdiction over advertising, franchises and business opportunities. Deals involving interstate promotion of land sales are regulated by the federal Department of Housing and Urban Development.

By contacting the appropriate regulatory organization, you can generally find out whether the firm or person is properly registered to engage in that type of business and whether any public disciplinary actions have been taken against them.

- **Write or phone law enforcement agencies.**

  Whether or not a person or firm is subject to the scrutiny of a regulatory organization, the fact is that fraud is against the law in every state of the nation. And if it involves interstate commerce--including the use of the mails or phone lines--federal criminal statutes apply. If an investment sounds suspicious, check with the appropriate agency. They may be able to furnish information or conduct an investigation of their own.

The office of the local public prosecutor, the state attorney general, and the state securities administrator. Someone in the local courthouse should be able to give you names, addresses and phone numbers.

If the mails are used in promoting or operating a phony investment scheme, federal Postal Inspectors want to know about it. The postmaster in your community can put you in touch with them. Fraud involving any form of interstate commerce is also of interest to the Federal Bureau of Investigation. The nearest office should be listed in your phone directory. The listing on the inside back cover of this booklet includes headquarter addresses of the U.S. Postal Inspector in Charge and the FBI.

Sure it can take some time, effort and possibly expense to thoroughly check out an investment proposal, but if you have any doubt about whether it's worth the trouble, talk with people who didn't and wish they had!

Finally, Don't Lose Touch with Your Money

The need to exercise good financial sense doesn't stop once you've decided to invest. It's possible, all your precautions notwithstanding, that you may have turned your money over to a swindler. It's also possible that what didn't start out to be a swindle may turn into one if the promoter finds himself in financial trouble or with too many poor investments on his hands. That can lead to cover-up bookkeeping or, worse yet, a decision by the promoter to take flight with what's left of his customers' money.

It's important to continuously monitor your investments and to be alert for any telltale signs that things aren't quite the way they should be. The person who sold you the investment, for example, may suddenly become inaccessible--continuously tied up on the telephone or unwilling to return your calls, busy with clients, or out-of-town on important business matters. Or various documents or accounting statements you were promised don't arrive. Or information you do receive is vague or at variance from what you had been led to expect. Or money that was supposed to have been paid to you isn't received, and instead of checks you get excuses.

If you become suspicious or overly uncomfortable with an investment you've made--and if you are unable to totally resolve your concerns --the best thing you can do is try to get out of it. And do so as

"Money was never a big motivation for me, except as a way to keep score. The real excitement is playing the game."

– Donald Trump

quickly as possible. That means demanding your money back, accompanied, if necessary, by threats to contact authorities.

You might or might not get it. The best you can hope for, if indeed there's fraud involved, is that the swindler may decide to refund your money rather than risk having you blow the whistle while he is still on the prowl for new investors. If that happens, consider yourself more fortunate than most.

Be aware, if you do decide to try and get a refund, that the person who was smooth-talking enough to get your money in the first place will unleash all his skills to persuade you to leave it with him. No doubt, he will have some answer for all of your concerns. And some explanation for all apparent irregularities. And, no doubt you will be told that backing out now would be anything from contractually illegal to a terrible financial mistake. Swindlers figure that every once in a while some of their more fidgety investors simply have to be reconvinced. He may tell you that you are so close to making really big money, or the investment now looks even more profitable than originally expected.

Believe him at your own peril.

If you do insist on a refund of your investment, insist on it immediately. Ask to pick it up yourself, or offer to pay the cost of having it sent by overnight mail or wired directly to your bank. Don't settle for "it will take a week or two" or "the check is in the mail." As everyone knows, checks seem to be lost more often than any other type of mail!

If you don't get your investment back (and chances are you won't), or even if you do and still suspect a swindle, report it promptly to the appropriate authorities and regulatory officials. They may be able to conduct an investigation and, if called for, seek legal action to impound whatever funds the firm still has.

Bottom line, the unfortunate reality is that very few victims of investment fraud ever again see a cent of their money. It's also a reality that the business of swindling will continue to flourish as long as unwary investors provide prey for unscrupulous promoters. Hopefully, the information in this booklet--if heeded--will help to assure that a swindler's next fortune won't be made at the expense of your misfortune.

Winning: What it takes to be Number One

I taped this speech to my mirror and read it every morning for my first two years in the business.

Winning is not a sometime thing it is an all the time thing. You don't win once in a while. You don't do things right once and awhile; you do them right all the time. Winning is a habit. Unfortunately so is losing.

There is no room for second place. There is only one place in my game, and that's first place. There is a second place bowl game but it is a game for losers played by losers. It is and it has always been an American zeal to be first in anything that we do, and to win, and to win, and to win.

Every time a football player goes to ply his trade he's got to play from the ground up – from the soles of his feet right up to his head. Every inch of him has to play. Some guys play with their heads. That's OK. You've got to be smart to be number one in any business. But more importantly, you've got to play with every fiber of your body. If you're lucky enough to find a guy with a lot of head and a lot of heart, he's never going to come off the field second.

Running a football team is no different than running any other kind of organization – an army, a political party or a business. The principles are the same. The object is to win – to beat the other guy. Maybe that sounds hard or cruel. I don't think it is.

It is a reality of life that men are competitive and the most competitive games draw the most competitive men. That's why they are there. To compete. To know the rules and objectives when they get in the game. The object is to win fairly and squarely, by the rules – but to win.

And in truth, I've never known a man worth his salt who in the long run, deep down in his heart, didn't appreciate the grind, the discipline. There is something in good men that really yearns for discipline and the harsh reality of head to head combat.

I don't say these things because I believe in the "Brute" nature of man or that men must be brutalized to be combative. I believe in God and I believe in human decency. But I firmly believe that any man's finest hour – his greatest fulfillment to all he holds dear – is that moment when he has to work his heart out in a good cause and he's exhausted on the field of battle – victorious.

– Vincent Lombardi –

Great Grandparenting

Building and Maintaining a Strong Relationship With Your Grandchild

This chapter is from an information packet sent to me by an investment firm I did business with in the mid 1990's. Although it has little to do with investing your money, it sure has gone a long way toward bringing some of my clients and their grandchildren closer together. Since my grandfather, Tim Murphy, and I were very close and I learned a lot of great things from my grandfather, I am presenting you this chapter with good wishes for you and your grandchildren!

The relationship between grandparent and grandchild is special and unique. For children, the attachment can be powerful and emotionally intense. For grandparents, the relationship allows you to relax and enjoy yourself as you provide love and nurturing to a child. Like many parents, you may have been so busy raising your child the first time around that you couldn't slow down and relish the experience. Now you have another chance to savor the rewards.

Grandparents have always had plenty of love and experience to share, yet over the years, the image of the stereotypical grandparent has changed. Rather than rocking in a chair on the porch, most grandparents are active-working, traveling, and pursuing their dreams. Whether you live a continent away or within the same house, the following are some ideas for building and maintaining a strong relationship with your grandchild.

The Bond Between Grandparent and Grandchild

Psychologists have noted that the bond between grandparent and grandchild is a pure, emotionally uncomplicated form of love. Often this love is freer and more playful than the love parents feel for their children. Grandparents themselves say it best-they report that being a grandparent affords them the pride and pleasure of raising a child, without the burdens and worries. For children, grandparents provide an emotional safety net. Children who grow up enjoying a strong relationship with their grandparents report feeling more emotionally secure than children who lack this bond. And these children demonstrate healthier attitudes towards older people, whom they've learned to love and respect firsthand. Teenagers and young adults often say that their one-on-one relationships with their grandparents helped shape them in significant ways.

Some child development experts have suggested that unlike a parent, a grandparent can appreciate a child's good qualities without feeling responsible for their bad behavior or shortcomings. Through their love, grandparents can foster a sense of self-esteem in their grandchildren. In addition, grandparents offer the child an identity within the extended family and a place in history.

Shared Activities

When planning activities for your grandchild, it's best to keep it simple. You don't need to plan elaborate entertainment spectaculars; the time you spend with your grandchild is enough. Involve him/her in your own favorite activities; fishing, baking, stamp collecting, swimming, raking leaves, gardening, and reading are some perennial favorites. In particular, children enjoy learning from their grandparents.

Teaching your grandchild to bake a pie or to grow tomatoes is rewarding for you both. Or try taking him/her to your workplace or where you volunteer to teach him/her about adult life and what you do.

You can even make a simple chore like a trip to the grocery store into an adventure. For instance, you might talk about where the products on the shelves are primarily eaten. Explain that tortillas are common in Mexico, spaghetti is a favorite in Italy, and Gouda cheese comes from Amsterdam.

When you get home, you might locate these countries on a map together. In this way, an ordinary trip to the supermarket can be made appealing and even educational.

Young children (under age seven) in particular, enjoy repetition. If you always visit the zoo together, they will associate you with this entertaining outing.

Here are some tips for making the most of your time with your grandchild:

- Spend time one-on-one with each grandchild. Family gatherings can be hectic times. Try to make a date to spend time with each of your grandchildren individually.

- Find a hobby to share. If you and your grandchild don't already share a common interest, choose one and make it your own. Collecting postcards or stamps, reading, and taking long walks are activities that most adults and children enjoy.

- Travel together. Grandparents often have time to travel. If you have the resources, you might plan a trip with your grandchild.

- Lend your grandchild an inexpensive camera. Encourage your grandchild to photograph your times together. You can both cherish the photos when you're apart.

Communicating With Your Grandchild

The time parents and children spend together is often hectic. As a grandparent, when you're with your grandchild you can usually slow down and focus on each other. Take this time to ask your grandchild questions about his/her life. Find out what she's learning at school, who his/her friends are, and what types of interests she is developing. Be sure to share information about your own life. Tell your grandchild about your job, volunteer work, travel, and friends; sometimes children are surprised to hear what active, busy people their grandparents are. Don't forget to talk about your past, too, telling stories about your childhood or the child's parent growing up. Above all, communicate your love for him/her. Here are some ideas for communicating with your grandchild:

- Accept your grandchild's feelings. Often, parents and grandparents try to smooth over painful emotions by saying, "That's nothing! You'll forget about it tomorrow." Take your grandchild's feelings seriously, even if you strongly suspect they'll be short-lived.

- Try not to pressure your grandchild. Even saying "I wish that you could come stay with me" or "Why don't you write me more often?" That might make your grandchild feel guilty or resentful that you want something that he or she has no control over giving.

- Avoid being critical. Being a good listener is more valuable than lecturing a grandchild about how to behave, which is the parents' responsibility. Try not to compare children to their parents or to your other grandchildren.

- Take your grandchild's concerns seriously. Listen carefully to what your grandchild is saying, and then respond to his/her questions or concerns.

Handing Down Traditions

You don't have to be a famous inventor or the first woman to sit on the Supreme Court to have valuable lessons to pass on to your grandchildren. Tell stories about the accomplishments of relatives, like the first family member to attend college or someone who lived through a particularly interesting chapter of history.

Tales of achievement foster self-esteem by helping children to discover heroes within their own family. For children, the past seems exotic. In fact, many children and teens find it unimaginable that people could exist without such everyday technology as televisions, microwaves, answering machines, and computers. Simply describing the house where you grew up and what things you had (and didn't have) may be interesting to your grandchild. Here are a few ways that you can pass on traditions to your grandchild:

- Create a family "museum," in which your child can look at old photos, jewelry, china, and other treasures.

- Host a family "film" festival. Show home movies, videos, or slides from different family branches. Remember the pop corn!

- Tell stories about your grandchild's mother or father-as a child.

- Write a brief family history. Invite your grandchild to draw it.

- Make a family tree together.

- Share family stories, jokes, and recipes.

Staying in Touch With Your Grandchild

Once upon a time, most family members lived in the same community, or at least in close proximity to one another. Today, families need to come up with new and imaginative ways to stay emotionally close, even when geographically far apart. It is important to start developing a relationship with far-flung grandchildren as soon as possible.

Begin talking to your grandchild on the phone when she is only six months old, saying what you'd say if you were actually holding the infant. You might sing a lullaby, tell your grandchild who this is, or just say "I love you, dear."

Visits are a lifeline for long-distance grandparents. Like some grandparents, you may prefer having one child visit at a time. If you have several grand-children visiting at once, you may feel divided and end up spending precious time refereeing among competing siblings. Remember to plan your grand-child's visits carefully, even though you should be flexible about modifying plans to suit everyone's moods.

Discussing plans in advance is one way to create excitement about future visits. Although these tips are designed for long-distance grandparents, they are excellent ways to strengthen your relationship with your grandchild, no matter where she lives:

- Make a tape or video. Until children are nine or ten years old, they are not especially good at talking on the telephone. Send a tape or video of yourself delivering a message to your grandchild.

- Write letters. Who says letter-writing is a dying art? It's still a vital connection for grandchildren and grandparents! Children rarely get mail and enjoy the thrill of seeing their own names on an envelope. Asking questions and enclosing a self-addressed, stamped envelope are ways to encourage a written response.

- Record yourself telling bedtime stories. You may want to ask your grandchild or his/her parent for some favorite stories, or you could just tape children's stories that you enjoy. This is one way of being present in your grandchild's life on a daily (or nightly) basis.

- Give your grandchild a map. Be sure to mark both of your homes on the map. You might send your grandchild books and articles about your community to prepare him/her for future visits.

- Send small gifts along with a message. Pipe cleaners, balloons, and flower seeds are educational and inexpensive gifts for children ages three to six. Most older children enjoy magic tricks, recipes, and colored pencils.

- Write postcards. Send each child his/her own postcard with a simple, personal message. (Pictures of animals, planes, and cartoons are generally big successes with children.)

To make your visits as memorable as possible, speak with your grandchild on the phone before you see each other face to face. Be sure to emphasize how happy you will be to see your grandchild once again. Building and maintaining a relationship with your grandchild takes planning and foresight, but the rewards are so great that they are impossible to measure. Your closeness bridges the generation gap and enriches your grandchild's life, as well as your own.

Resources for Further Information

Isbister, Ruth. *Grandparents Don't Just Babysit.* Toronto, Ontario: Deneau Publishers, 1989.

LeShan, Eda. *Grandparenting in a Changing World.* New York, NY: Newmarket Press, 1993.

Stoop, Jan and Betty Southard. *The Grandmother Book.* Nashville, TN: Thomas Nelson Publishers, 1993.

Wassermann, Selma. *The Long Distance Grandmother.* Point Roberts, WA: Hartley & Marks, 1988.

For More Information

To learn more about estate planning strategies, talk with an experienced estate planning attorney or financial advisor, and check out the following resources.

A list of names, addresses and phone numbers of organizations and agencies noted in this book:

AARP:

(www.aarp.org / 1-800-424-3410) Ask for a copy of Product Report: Wills & Living Trusts. AARP does not sell or endorse living trust products.

The American Bar Association

(www.abanet.org/publiced/publicpubs.html / 312-988-5522)
Service Center, 541 N. Fairbanks Ct., Chicago, IL. 60611

Council of Better Business Bureaus, Inc.

(http://www.bbb.org / 703-276-0100)
4200 Wilson Blvd., Suite 800, Arlington, VA 22203-1838;

The National Academy of Elder Law Attorneys, Inc.

(http://www.naela.org / 520-881-4005)
1604 North Country Club Rd., Tucson, AZ 85716;

The National Consumer Law Center, Inc.

(http://www.consumerlaw.org / 617-523-8010)
18 Tremont St., Ste. 400, Boston, MA 02108-2336

Commodity Futures Trading Commission

2033 K St., N.W.
Washington, D.C. 20581
202.254.6387

Federal Bureau of Investigation

Justice Department
9th St. and Pennsylvania Ave.,
N.W. Washington, D.C. 20535
202.234.3691

Federal Trade Commission

6th St. & Pennsylvania Ave., N.W.
Washington, D.C. 20580
202.326.3650

Housing and Urban Development Department

Interstate Land Sales Registration
HUD Building
451 7th St., S.W. Room 6262
Washington, D.C. 20410-8000
202.755.0502

National Association of Securities Dealers

1735 K St., N.W.
Washington, D.C. 20006
202.728.8044

National Futures Association

200 W. Madison, Suite 1600
Chicago, IL 60606-3447
Toll Free: 800.621.3570
In IL: 800.572.9400

Securities and Exchange Commission

450 Fifth St., N.W.
Washington, D.C. 20006
202.728.8233

United States Postal Service

Chief Postal Inspector
Room 3021
Washington, D.C. 20260-2100
202.268.4267

Prepared as service to the investing public by:

National Future Association
200 West Madison Street, Suite 1600
Chicago, Illinois 60606-3447
Toll-free: 800.621.3570
In IL: 800.572.9400

Where to Complain:

Federal Trade Commission
(www.ftc.gov) / 1-877-FTC-HELP (1-877-382-4357)

The FTC works for the consumer to prevent fraudulent, deceptive and unfair business practices in the marketplace and to provide information to help consumers spot, stop and avoid them. To file a complaint, or to get free information on any of 150 consumer topics, call toll-free at the above number or use the online complaint form. The FTC enters Internet, telemarketing, and other fraud-related complaints into Consumer Sentinel, a secure, online database available to hundreds of civil and criminal law enforcement agencies in the U.S. and abroad.

Books:

Plan Your Estate
Denis Clifford and Cora Jordan, Nolo Press
Life Advice® readers save up to 40% on the purchase of Nolo products by calling 1-800-728-3555 and mentioning DMET or visit www.nolo.com.

The American Bar Association Guide to Wills and Estates
Times Books ($13)

Baby Boomer Retirement: 65 Simple Ways to Protect Your Future
(Second Edition) Don Silver, Adams-Hall Publishing ($14.95)
Life Advice® price ($10) Price includes shipping and handling. To order call 1-800/888-4452 and mention Life Advice® or send a check payable to Adams-Hall Publishing, P.O. Box 491002, Dept. LA, Los Angeles, CA 90049.

Pamphlets from the Federal Government:

Consumer Information Center Catalog
(www.pueblo.gsa.gov / 1-888/8-PUEBLO)
The quarterly Consumer Information Center Catalog lists more than 200 helpful federal publications.

Internet:

www.nolo.com
Online legal information and advice

www.freeadvice.com
Easy to use site for legal information

www.aaepa.com / 1-800/846-1555
Academy of Estate Planning Attorneys

www.actec.org / 310/398-1888
American College of Trust and Estate Counsel

www.netplanning.com / 1-800/638-8681
National Network of Estate Planning Attorneys

www.courttv.com
The folks at CourtTV have put together a terrific site on all things legal.

www.irs.gov
You can find very helpful info from this user-friendly site. Check it out for answers
to your trust-related tax questions.

www.metlife.com
A well-designed program for financial security begins with life insurance.